Transcripts from the Past

The Sir John Barrow Monument

The Story of Hoad
1848 -1859

Jack Layfield (ed.)

© Handstand Press
48 Market Street, Ulverston, LA12 7LS

First published in 2005 by
Handstand Press,
48 Market Street, Ulverston LA12 7LS

All rights reserved. No part of this publication may be reproduced, stored in a retrieval system, or transmitted, in any form or by any means, without the prior permission in writing of Handstand Press.

The publishers make no representation, express or implied, with regard to the accuracy of the information contained in this book and cannot accept any legal responsibility for any errors or omissions that may take place.

ISBN 0-955200-90-3

Cover Design by Martin Chester (design_jack@btinternet.com)
Printed in Great Britain by Finger prints, Barrow in Furness, Cumbria.

Acknowledgements
All photographs in this publication are courtesy of Jennifer Snell.
Thanks to The North West Evening Mail for permission to publish.
Gratitude to Mr. Soulby for recording so meticulously the events of the day.

Introduction

In 2004, I with a friend, Rob Mckeever co-authored a history book, the *The Industrial Archaeology of South Ulverston*. During one of my many visits to Barrow Reference Library, I came across old newspapers of Ulverston, produced by Soulby's Advertiser. Soulby Ltd, a long established firm of printers in the town, first published the *Soulby's Ulverston Advertiser* as a monthly in October 1847. Within the year it was coming out fortnightly and then, from Thursday 10th. October 1848, it became a weekly. I very quickly realised what a wealth of information these old newspapers contained and an idea came to me that they would make interesting booklets tracing the different aspects of the history of Ulverston. With this in mind, I contacted *The North West Evening Mail*, the papers current owner, and they kindly gave their permission.

The articles transcribed here have been taken from facsimile copies of *Soulby's Ulverston Advertiser*. Every effort has been made to reproduce the grammar and spelling (including italics) as it appeared in the original. However, some of the copy is indecipherable and where this is the case a dotted line is shown.

I have chosen to start with the story of the Sir John Barrow Monument, locally known as "The Hoad" (the name of the hill on which it stands). Like most Ulverstonians, I have an affection for the Monument; so much so, that for a period in the 1980's, I and my family took on the caretaking duties there. It is also appropriate now as a group of local people, aptly named The Friends of Hoad, are actively raising funds for its repair. So I thought this a good time to put together the story of its early life for all with interest and affinity to the Monument to read.

Soulby's Ulverston Advertiser followed the construction of the Sir John Barrow Memorial in great detail. Mr. Soulby, the paper's editor, was a member of the Ulverston Committee, responsible for liaising with the Admiralty in London to manage the project. The years covered in this account, 1848-1859, are full of incident.

There are disputes over funding; debates about the choice of design and building material; an accident on-site and problems with vandalism. But there is much to celebrate as well from the grand feelings expressed following the death of Sir John Barrow through to the celebrations at the laying of the foundation stone and the eventual opening of the Monument. I hope you enjoy reading the story of the Sir John Barrow Monument as much as I have enjoyed researching it.
Jack Layfield. December 2005.

Transcripts from the Past

The Sir John Barrow Monument
The Story of Hoad
1848-1859

Soulby's Ulverston Advertiser

30th November 1848
Death of our eminent Townsman, Sir John Barrow, Bart, LLD; F.R.S. &c.
We have the painful duty this week of announcing to our readers the sudden death of our celebrated townsman Sir John Barrow, who, for a period of forty years was secretary to the Admiralty. The events which constituted the history of the distinguished Baronet are of an extremely interesting and varied character, as all who have read his excellent Autobiography, published last year, have occasion to know; but as these events are so well known to most of the individuals residing in the vicinity of his birth-place, it will not be necessary for us to recapitulate them.

The life of this eminent individual, - of whom as a town, we have so much occasion to be proud, - affords an exemplary illustration of what may be effected by the possession of brilliant talents, perseverance and industry, when united to a high moral character.

Of comparatively humble origin, and without possessing those advantages of education, and family connexion, which are enjoyed by many, he exalted himself by the unaided effort of his intellectual, and moral abilities out of that sphere in which he had been placed by birth, to an elevated and highly honourable position, - a position which afforded full scope for the display of his singular talents, and the development of his extraordinary capabilities. Without influence and without patronage, he gradually drew towards himself those who were capable of assisting him, until at length he was elevated to a position, in which he could number amongst his friends those who either by birthright or talent were the most illustrious men of the day. Scions of royalty, statesmen and peers, with those who had distinguished themselves by their literary abilities, were amongst his daily and intimate acquaintances; while by his Sovereign, his moral probity, and extraordinary talents were cordially acknowledged, and properly appreciated.

The life of Sir John Barrow impresses one with a more favourable opinion of humanity than gloomy misanthropes, - those gross impugners of our species, - would have us entertain. For, while we see surpassing, but still unostentatious merit thus honoured and appreciated, as well as rewarded, we cannot help giving the world some credit at least for its discernment, and sense of justice. We see at once that a kindly and generous disposition begets the like estimable characteristics in those with whom it comes in contact; and that the world is not so insensible as some would have us believe it to be, to the claims of high intellectual merit, when suitably supported by corresponding moral qualifications. We see, in fine, that genius is still rewarded, and that the good are ever valued and esteemed by those whose good opinion is worth possessing.

But while we thus cordially admit that credit is due to the world for thus perceiving and appreciating distinguished merit, we must not forget to pay our tribute of praise to him who could thus raise himself out of obscurity to an exalted station in society, and build for himself out of the materials which his own abilities afforded, an extensive and valuable reputation, -the best monument which could possibly be erected to the memory of a human being. Nor must we forget to mention, that amidst all the labours which this position entailed upon the esteemed subject of this memoir, and amidst all the successes and triumphs which attended these labours, Sir John never forgot the humble spot that gave him birth. In a letter, which the writer of this article had recently the honour to receive from his celebrated fellow townsman, Sir John warmly stated the "affectionate interest" as, he himself expressed it, which he then felt in all that was connected with his native town; and we learn, that by his will, the usual annual subscription which he has been in the habit of contributing for a long series of years in support of *"The Sunday School"* will be continued; and "the cottage" at Dragley-beck, recently purchased by a gentleman of this town, and by him transferred to John Barrow, Esq. is to be given over in perpetuity to trustees, the rent to be appropriated towards the education of the children of the poor, of the above mentioned school. Thus not only in life, but in the "hour, and article of death" he has remembered the place of his nativity. And we are well assured of this, that if we were not forgotten by Sir John, he will never be forgotten by us, but that his memory will continue to be cherished, and his example held up as heretofore for the imitation of all those who, born in the same locality, may be gifted with some portion, however small, of the same talents which served to distinguish him in life, and which will, we cannot doubt, effectually perpetuate his name and his virtues to posterity. We well remember the time when a boy, and while attending the school at which he who is the subject of this brief notice received the rudiments of education, when any one of the pupils had performed some meritorious action the worthy master laying his hand upon his head, would remind him that "The School" had already produced *one Sir John Barrow*, and would hold out hopes of the possibility that it might produce another. And thus it is that a great and estimable character serves to inspire others with a laudable ambition to walk in his steps, and acquire honours similar to those which he has acquired. The name of Sir John Barrow has long been a houschold word amongst us; and although he who bore it is departed, his memory still lingers lovingly about our hearts and our firesides, and will continue to be cherished by our children, and our children's children, through succeeding generations.

Sir John having expressly desired that his funeral might be conducted with the strictest privacy, his three sons, his old friends Sir Geo. Staunton, Sir Henry Brodie, and his late colleague Mr. Croker, we believe would be the only attendants. Yesterday was the day appointed for the internment, which was here observed by tolling of bells of the old Church, and a blue ensign, half pole high, waved over the cottage in which he was born.

27th September 1849
To the Editor of the *Ulverston Advertiser*. Sir, -The best and purest feelings of our nature prompt us to pay respect to departed ability and worth; and this instructive tendency of our moral constitution is quite independent of our particular kind of excellence, for which the individual, whose memory we are desirous of honouring, was distinguished in life. It equally holds good in the case of the upright and conscientious statesmen, of the self-denying and laborious Divine; and of the man who, by a combination of talent and industry, and good principle, has raised himself from small beginnings to wealth, and rank, and reputation.

In common, accordingly, with the great majority of the inhabitants of Ulverston and its neighbourhood, I rejoiced when it was announced that a Testimonial was about to be erected in honour of the late Sir John Barrow. A considerable sum of money, I understand, has already been raised for this purpose; and it is confidently expected that further subscriptions, in aid of this laudable undertaking, will still be forth coming. The main difficulty, then, being surmounted - the *nature* of the Testimonial to be erected only remains for decision. The friends of the late excellent Secretary of the Admiralty, resident in London, have thought that the raising of a Pillar, or Column, in the neighbourhood of his native place (which might serve as a sea-mark) would be a fitting and appropriate shape for the Testimonial to assume. But after a careful survey by a scientific eye of the various eminences near the town which command a view of Morecambe Bay, it is now admitted that the erection of a column of this kind would not be of the slightest use to mariners. I trust, therefore, that the more influential subscribers may be induced to abandon this project, and to adopt in its stead some memorial of a more useful character.*

The mind of Sir John Barrow was eminently of a *practical* character; and no one can have read his very interesting autobiography without seeing that, to this peculiarity, his remarkable success in life may be principally attributed. It seems but fitting, therefore, that the proposed Testimonial should accord in some degree with the character of the distinguished individual in whose honour it is to be erected. But still the question recurs, of what *nature* should it be? If I may, without presumption, offer a suggestion to the subscribers, I should propose that the money raised be applied to increasing the endowment of Townbank School, in which this worthy Baronet was taught the rudiments of his education, and in which his peculiar talent received its earliest development.

I need not stay to point out how much the inhabitants of Ulverston would be benefited, in a moral and social point of view, by raising the character of the instruction imparted in that school. For though there might be trained there no future Secretaries of the Admiralty to reflect credit on their native town; yet, sure I am, that many a youth, poor and humble though his origin might be, would, (through God's blessing on the sound and practical education which he there received,) become useful and valuable members of society, and pass through life respected and esteemed by their fellow citizens.

Perhaps I ought to apologize to you for the length to which my communication has extended; but, believing that many of your readers will concur with me in the suggestion which I have taken the liberty of making. I feel certain that you will readily give publicity to this feeble attempt, to procure a substantial benefit to the whole community.

I am, Mr. Editor, yours faithfully,
N.N.

[* Here we beg to differ from our respected correspondent. We believe that he is labouring under some misapprehension in reference first to the *object* which the promoters of the proposed erection have in view; and, secondly, in reference to the *qualifications* of the several sites in the locality. With regards to the first the *principal* aim of the supporters of the project, is to make the Column, or Tower, serve as a *memento* of the late Sir John Barrow; - the *secondary* aim is to make it serve the purpose of a *sea-mark*, to facilitate the navigation of Morecambe Bay. With regards to the second it has never, as yet, been objected that Hoad is not in every way fitted to serve the most important of the purposes which we have already enumerated, namely, that of an eligible site for the intended *memento,* while its unfitness to serve as a sea-marker has never, that we have heard of, been strenuously asserted. -Ed. U.A.]

October 4th 1849

In our last week's publication our readers would see a letter bearing the signature of "N. N.," upon which we beg to offer one or two observations. In the first place we would remark that the tenor and tone of our correspondent's communication are benevolent in the extreme; and that therefore the hope which it expresses that the influential subscribers may be induced to abandon their projected erection to the memory of the late esteemed Sir John Barrow arises from no false notion of economy, and no undue estimation of the relative value of money. On the contrary the writer regards the wish to pay honour and respect to the memory of departed merit, as "one of the purest feelings of our nature," and proceeds to signify the pleasure with which he, in common with "the great majority of the inhabitants of Ulverston" heard the announcement that a "Testimonial was about to be erected in honour of the late Sir John Barrow."

It is therefore not to the *Testimonial* that he objects, nor to the purpose for which the funds have been subscribed, but only to the manner of their application -to the *form* which it is intended that the Testimonial shall assume; and while he objects to the erection of a tower or column, he suggests another mode in which the memory of the deceased Baronet may be preserved, that would, as he conceives, be at once more useful and beneficial in its character, and more in harmony with the whole life of him whom it is intended to honour. Before speaking of his *suggestion,* we must be allowed to say a word or two upon his *objections.*

And here it is necessary to be very brief; for we believe that the *ground* of his objections is as we stated in the foot-note that accompanied the letter in question, and arises solely from a "misapprehension of the object which the promoters of the proposed erection have in view" on the one hand, and misinformation in reference to the "qualifications of the several sites in the locality" on the other. It is evident that "N.N." supposes that because it has been asserted that there are no eminences in the neighbourhood which are *eminently* well qualified to serve the purpose of a sea-mark, therefore the scheme for the erection of the projected *memento* should be abandoned: -thus causing the *secondary* consideration to stand in the place of the *primary*, taking a *part* for the whole, and falling into the error of arguing from the *particular* to the *universal*. The memorial, whether it takes the form of a tower or a column, if erected upon Hoad, would not only be an embellishment to the town, but would be *practically useful* and serviceable in more senses than one. In the first place it would be a centre of attraction to the numerous visitors of the Lake-district, from almost every part of which it would be a conspicuous object in the distant horizon; and, by inducing these pleasure-seekers and curiosity-lovers to visit the town, it is scarcely necessary to add that its trade and commerce would be materially improved. In the next place it would serve as an object of emulation to the youths of the town and neighbourhood. It would show them what talent and ability can achieve when supported by habits of industry and temperance. It would be a lasting indication of that esteem and respect which merit inspires, not only through life, and in death, but of that honour which still continues to wait patiently on its memory, long after the grave has closed over the remains of the departed.

With regard to the *suggestion* of our correspondent we think it as benevolent in design, as would be beneficial in execution. It embraces at once the enlargement of the endowment of the Town Bank Grammar School, and the consequent improvement in the character of the education therein imparted. We say *consequent*, for although it cannot be said in every instance, that every fresh accession of wealth, like every successive acquisition in the liberal sciences.
"Emollit mores, nec sinit esse feros;"

yet, after all, gold is that necessary material which may be given in exchange for most other valuable commodities; and we have every reason to suppose that by making the stipend of the master liberal, we shall make liberal that which he imparts in exchange for the stipend. But then it surely does not follow that, in order to heighten the tone of the instruction communicated at the Town Bank School; the scheme for the erection of a monument to the memory of the late Sir John Barrow should be abandoned; or that the funds which have been collected for this purpose should be applied to any other object than that for which they were originally subscribed. It is certainly not a matter of necessity that, in order to improve the character of the school, we must forgo the advantages of the monument; or that, in order to possess the monument, we must throw a barrier in the way of the ultimate progression and advancement of the school. Sir John Barrow's Memorial, and the Town Bank Grammar School, are surely not two antagonistic elements, the coalescence or coagmentation of which is impossible; - the one may certainly exist without implying the destruction or abandonment of the other.

The excellency of the aim and object of our correspondent's communication is apparent to all; and has excited considerable pleasure in the minds of many. If the scheme be deemed practicable to improve the character of the education imparted at the Town Bank Grammar School, and thereby to confer a lasting benefit on the town and its vicinity, let all who are favourable to it - and surely there will be found none oppose it *by treating it with coldness* - contribute towards carrying the benevolent design into execution; and thus, instead of having one good thing we shall have the good doubled; and while the memorial will be an embellishment to the town, and will cause an influx of visitors to promote its commercial prosperity, the school, by imparting a more refined and elevated species of instruction, will confer *mental* embellishments to adorn the life and character of its future inhabitants.

27ᵗʰ December 1849

We hail with delight, the announcement, that Captain Washington, Tidal Harbour Commissioner, who was officially instructed to make a personal survey as to the site for a monument to be erected to the memory of the late Sir John Barrow, Bart., Assistant Secretary to the Admiralty, to combine the two-fold object of its being placed near to the birth-place of the deceased Baronet, and at the same time so situated as to be of practical utility as a sea-marker to vessels navigating Morecambe Bay, has reported the Hill of Hoad at Ulverston to be the proper site; and that the Committee in London, and Sir Frances Beaufort, Hydrographer to the Admiralty, have coincided in the report.

As to the suitability of the proposed site for the objects contemplated, there cannot, we are inclined to believe, be a second opinion. The Hill of Hoad commands a pleasing and uninterrupted view of the Cottage at Dragley Beck, in which the late Baronet was born, and is also contiguous to the Town Bank School, where Sir John received his earliest education -an institution in the welfare of which, he was throughout the course of his long life, greatly interested -and the churchyard, where repose his ancestral remains, is near the foot of Hoad.

The Hill of Hoad was also the favourite resort of Sir John in his youth as well for the purpose of healthful recreation as an appropriate scene for the indulgence of those contemplative habits to which he was naturally disposed.

The subscribers are no doubt anxious that the proposed erection should not in any way detract from the primary object contemplated; but that while it handed down the memory of Sir John Barrow to posterity, it should at the same time be made as useful as possible to navigation and science, in the promotion of which Sir John so eminently distinguished himself during his protracted and laborious life. In the furtherance of their praiseworthy object we beg leave to suggest an Observatory, Lighthouse, and a Signal or Telegraph Station, for each of which purposes the Hill of Hoad is well adapted.

The Hill of Hoad as a site for an Observatory, both for nautical and astronomical purposes, offers a most extensive field for telescopic power and range of vision. It commands nearly the whole of Morecambe Bay, not only from Greenodd, the extreme navigable part northward of the Ulverston Sands, -the port of Ulverston, Parkhead, Carkbeck, Conishead Bank, the offing at Bardsea, but on the Lancaster side, -Hestbank, Poulton Ring, Lancaster and the Lune, Fleetwood and the Wyre. Beyond the geographical limits of the Bay are seen the entrances to Lytham, Preston, and the Ribble, and in fine weather even as far as the mouth of the Mersey. The view would also command Piel Harbour, Walney, the entrance to the Duddon, and a portion of the coast and offing seawards in the direction of Bootle in Cumberland, and as far also as the mountains of the Isle of Man; whilst landward, the view commands Scawfell, Helvellyn, and others of that lofty range in the Lake district in the north - Ingleborough in Yorkshire, on the east, and Blackcombe in Cumberland, on the West. For astronomical objects, the view of the heavens is most extensive and magnificent and stellar observations there, could not fail to be of national importance. For the purpose of a Lighthouse, it would be visible to all points within the range of a segment of a circle of many miles radius, and would materially contribute in rendering Morecambe Bay safely navigable at night, and contribute much to the preservation of ships, and the lives of the crews. The light would also be serviceable to parties crossing the Sands, many lives having been lost for want of a beacon to guide their steps. It would also serve useful purposes to miners and others traversing the hills after sun-set, in the winter months. As a Telegraphic station, a communication might easily be established by way of Pile of Fouldrey by means of the Lighthouse there and Fleetwood, by which means the arrival and departure of vessels to and from Ulverston, and the various parts in the United Kingdom, might be communicated -thus accomplishing a most desirable object, not only important to the mercantile interest, but affording speedy information to the relatives and friends of the ships' crews, who, for want of a telegraphic communication are often kept in a state of painful suspense.

It might also be used for the purpose of magnetic and meteorological observations, investigations in which the late Sir John took a lively interest, especially Magnetical Science, with reference to the discovery of a North-west passage; and in the present state of Scientific enquiry, particularly with reference to the general received opinions that the poles of the earth are becoming more and more perpendicular to the Ecliptic, cannot fail to be considered as having a bearing of national importance.

31st December 1849
To the Editor of the *Ulverston Advertiser*. Mr. Editor, Sir. -The announcement having been just made, through the columns of your valuable paper, that the Hill of Hoad is fixed upon as the site of the Barrow Monument, I think it is a seasonable time to remind the inhabitants of Ulverstone, and the neighbourhood, that the project of planting certain rocky portions of the Hill with ornamental trees and shrubs, has not yet been carried out. If you, Mr. Editor, would only trouble yourself to give us a few strokes of your pen, in advocacy of so desirable a scheme, I am persuaded the good taste of the inhabitants of the neighbourhood would be at once enlisted in the cause, and that the needful funds would be easily obtained.

I may be wrong, but I do fancy Hoad is now capable of being made, at a light expense, one of the most attractive and delightful places in the Lake District; and those, whose good fortune has located them in Ulverston, either permanently or otherwise, may well afford to give a few shillings towards heightening the most natural beauties of this romantic hill. Other towns have their public walks and mountains, and artificial lakes, and wide-spreading woods and parks, but few towns can boast of anything like the Hill of Hoad, commanding, as it does, from its airy summit, the most varied and magnificent views -compared with which, those walks and lakes, and parks, though beautiful, are, indeed, tame and insignificant.

If it should be resolved upon, to plant any part of Hoad, it should be done, either next month, (the weather permitting,) or not till the latter end of the year, to ensure successful operations. Leaving the subject in your hands, I am, Mr. Editor,
Yours truly,
A LOVER OF THE PICTURESQUE.

24th January 1850
To the Editor of the *Ulverston Advertiser*. Sir, -In my last letter I endeavoured to show the importance of a Lighthouse on Hoad, to the shipping interests of Morecambe Bay. The importance of a Lighthouse on that eminence will appear from another consideration. To persons unacquainted with the peculiar position of Morecambe Bay, they will be surprised to learn that it is during one half of the twenty four hours a highway for ships, and the other half a highway for travellers, horsemen and pedestrians of all classes; hence, after sunset, a Lighthouse is as essential to the preservation of the lives of travellers when the tide is out, as it is to the safety of ships and crews when the tidal waters maintain their potent supremacy. This is a department of the question deeply interesting to every person in Lonsdale North of the Sands. Thousands every year cross the sands at all hours, and melancholy is the reflection, I believe, a year never passes, without some life being lost; and the question which I put with respect to our mariners, I repeat with respect to travellers -"would not a Lighthouse be a means of saving many a valuable life?" I alluded in my last to having "heard the frightful death-shrieks of mariners when drowning in the Bay;" that event will well illustrate the memory of the above question. One day, some eighteen years ago, four men, three of whom were sailors, were sent down the Bay in search of a missing anchor, to a spot, if I remember right, between Bardsea and Itridge-scar, about four miles from Ulverston. In the evening, which was thick and hazy on land, I and a companion were amusing ourselves in a field behind the church, when suddenly our sports were arrested by the most frightful cries I ever heard, which appeared to proceed from the adjoining field. This first impression was confirmed by our seeing the figure of a man in the garb of a sailor behind the hedge, who beckoned us.

Imagining that some foul deed was being perpetrated, we rushed through the hedge, but the figure had disappeared, and though we searched round several fields we could find no trace of the mariner, but we again heard a cry which appeared far away from us. Next morning the mystery was solved. The party I have mentioned were overtaken by the tide -the alarm was given, one man took the right direction landwards, and called to the others but, it being so dark and hazy, they knew not which way to take, and alas! as too frequently happens on the sands, instead of going land-wards, they rushed seawards and perished! The cries we heard were the combined death struggles of three brave fellows, for whom there was *no lamp to guide their feet*. I give this case from memory, as I heard the facts at the time, and I believe my statement is correct, for having heard the dying cries of the poor fellows, which even now ring in my ears, it made an impression on my mind never to be effaced.

I now come to the application of these remarks, by what means could a Lighthouse be made serviceable for travellers crossing the sands. I make no pretensions to any practical knowledge on the subject of Lighthouses, nor would I be guilty of the presumption of saying one word on the proper manifestation of a light on Hoad -that is a question entirely for the consideration of the eminent authorities at Trinity House. All I propose to do is to attempt, by a familiar and simple illustration, to awaken public attention to the subject; we are all interested in it, and we must certainly be prepared if we wish to enjoy so great a boon as a light specially adapted to facilitate our crossing the sands during the night, to contribute something to the support of that special object.
My proposal, which is purely by way of illustration, is that the Light-tower should be of a hexagonal form, and that the three sides of this hexagon fronting Morecambe Bay should be thus distinguished with colours A. B. C. three sides of a hexagon fronting the Bay in such a manner, say, that B. looks southward, showing a *white* light. A. looking westward, C. eastward, each showing a *red* light. Now suppose a traveller has lost his way on Lancaster sands, and galloping as he imagines in the direction of Kents-bank, he should find himself going in the direction of Pile

light which he recognizes. He turns and sees the light on Hoad, the red light C. with the white B. on the left hand - A. being partially visible. Now suppose at the extremity of the Cartmel peninsula the red light A. is lost sight of, the traveller has nothing to do but ride till the light A. is lost to view, and he to his infinite joy gains the land. Thus you perceive whatever the bearings of the coloured lights may be, a traveller in the dark, having previously acquainted himself with them, need never be at a loss which way to go to gain the land, and the light would always prevent any one going seawards.
W. B.

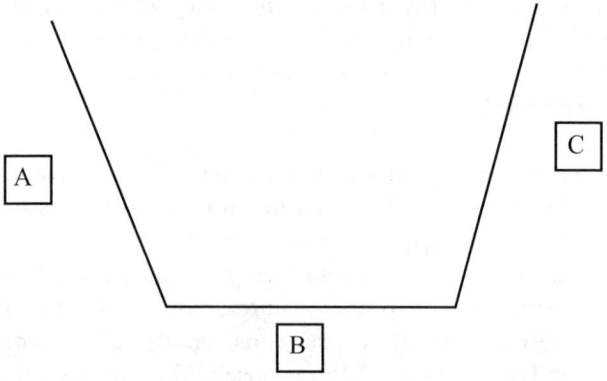

28th February 1850

We are informed that a letter was received on Tuesday last by Mr. W. Postlethwaite, Hoad Cottage, from John Barrow. Esq., of the Admiralty, stating that the Elder Brethren of the Trinity House have approved of the Hill of Hoad, as the site for the erection of a Monument to the aforementioned Sir John Barrow; on receipt of which Mr. Postlethwaite replied to Commander Beecher R. N. of the Hydrographic Office, confirming his previous offer made to Captain Washington that every facility should be given to them carrying out the views of the Committee. The Monument, which is to be 100 feet in height, will be commenced without further delay.

7th March 1850
Of the Barrow Testimonial the *Morning Herald* of Monday thus speaks: -"A committee of the Elder Brethren of the Trinity House (who, as we have already announced, have contributed £100 towards the Testimonial to the late Sir John Barrow, Bart.) having purposely visited Ulverston, have sanctioned the erection of a stone tower, 100 feet high, on the summit of Hoad Hill, an almost isolated, cone-shaped hill, rising abruptly to the north eastward of the town, its summit being 355 feet above the market-place of the town of Ulverston, and 435 feet above the mean level of the sea. Capt. Washington, R.N. who had previously inspected and reported upon the various sites in contemplation, considers the Hoad admirably adapted, from its natural form, to bear a tower on its summit. As a sea-mark it is likely in many ways to prove highly beneficial to navigation, and also to be made available as a leading mark from Fleetwood to Bardsea. Many of the associations of the inhabitants of Ulverston are connected with the Hoad, and it is their favourite resort on all holidays. Immediately at its foot lies Ulverston canal, one great source of the prosperity of the town, and where a short time since the traffic exceeded 60,000 tons of shipping a year. From the summit of Hoad the village of Dragley Beck, and the cottage in which Sir John Barrow was born, are distinctly visible. The Town Bank School, at which he was educated; the old parish church at which he worshipped; and the grave-yard in which his parents rest, stand on the rising ground leading up to Hoad, which was the favourite resort of his boyhood.

The selection of this site seems to be most appropriate, and cannot but be gratifying to the friends who have subscribed to this most useful undertaking, the funds for which already amount to upwards of £800. The amount is not so large as we could wish; but we trust that our townsmen will shake off the apathy which has so long held them back from aiding in the good work of raising the character of their native town, by placing it on an equal footing with other towns of its size and standing, and which can only be done by making it worthy the notice of men of science and attractive to pleasure seekers. Would it not then, we ask them, be as well were they to call a public meeting, and form a committee, who, by corresponding with the committee in London, and explaining the views of the inhabitants, the Tower may be made the means of local attraction by serving as a place of resort for recreation and amusement.

7th March 1850
The Proposed Museum For Ulverston and the Barrow Testimonial
To the Editor of the *Ulverston Advertiser*. Sir: -The great delight of a pleasure-seeking tourist, who has chosen the Lake district for his route, is to climb the highest mountain, to perambulate the margin of a lake, to sail upon its glass-like water, to make excursions to waterfalls, to gaze upon the ruins of an abbey, or the crumbling walls of an ancient castle. A locality famed only for its tradition, its legends, or its historical associations, possesses no charms for him. His object is to see *the lions* of the country through which he is travelling; and consequently he hurries over the intermediate distance, for he dreads a wet day. He has no notion of being confined to an inn in a strange town, with no other amusement than to watch the rain dashing "in gusty splashes against the window, trickling down the panes, or collecting in large uncomfortable looking drops on the frames." He has learned from his hand or guide book, the best route to take, the object of most note, and where to halt. And what do the guide books say of Ulverston? Simply that it is a flourishing market town and port, most pleasantly situated near the beautiful bay of Morecambe, and is nearly environed by hills. True -but will the scenery of Ulverston bear comparison with that which the traveller beheld as he approached the lakes, or feed his imagination with the scenes of bygone years, as when he gazed upon the ruins of Furness Abbey? Certainly not. It must be admitted, then, that Ulverston, in itself, possesses little or no attraction, either for the excursionist, the man of science, the scholar, or the romantic pedestrian. Hence is it, that so few lake visitors make a point of staying in the town longer than is really necessary to take a slight refreshment, or obtain a fresh conveyance. The ground between Coniston or Newby Bridge and Furness Abbey is hurried over as quickly as possible; and I am surprised that no effort has before been made to induce tourists to

make Ulverston, at least, a halting place for a few days. There is an old proverb, "better late than never," and now that the opportunity has occurred of doing so, I trust the inhabitants will not let it slip. I allude to the proposed Museum, in the Athenaeum, and Barrow Testimonial. And what town, I would ask, commands greater facilities than our own for forming a Museum! How many valuable relics of antiquity, found in the neighbourhood, have been lost to us by being disposed of elsewhere, which if a Museum had been in existence, would, most likely, have been brought for sale, or forwarded as gifts. Even specimens of the iron ore and copper ores of our mines would, of themselves, form no mean collection; "moreover the district presents a greater variety of geological features than any other of the same extent, and abounds with fossils. Occasionally, too, rare and beautiful species of fish are captured by fishermen; and stone hammers and other weapons of the Celts are often found." These are but few of the advantages which Ulverston possesses of carrying out the object in view. It will also confer a great lasting benefit upon the town, and a more fitting time than the present could not have been selected for the undertaking, when the Monument to the memory of Sir John Barrow is to be erected on the Hill of Hoad, which in itself, must prove a source of great attraction to the lake tourists, and consequently bring a large influx of strangers to the town, who will most assuredly, avail themselves of the opportunity afforded them of paying a visit to the Ulverston Museum. If I am rightly informed it is the intention of the directors of the Athenaeum to expend a portion of the proceeds, arising from the Bazaar and Exhibition, upon glass cases and other fixtures suitable for the preservation of such presents as have already been received, and which may hereafter be made. The remainder will, I believe, be applied to the purchase of books for the library of the Museum.
A LOVER OF TRUTH.

4th April 1850
We cannot but think, that a great mistake has been committed in leaving to the contractors, for this building, the choice of stone, moulding and dressed work excepted, which are to consist of Lancaster freestone. With all due deference to the Elder Brethren

of the Trinity House -whose cheerful and liberal response to the application made to them for their assistance, we have not forgotten -the Committee in London, and the Architect, we beg leave to offer our humble opinion that this part of the agreement is an oversight. It may not be know to them that there exists, on the very site on which the tower is to be built, a rock of very soft material, as may be seen in the excavation already commenced. In fact, it is of too soft a nature to withstand for any length of time, exposure to rough weather. With the amount of the tender accepted, we have nothing whatever to do. But it must be admitted, that the contractors have an undoubted right, a right which their contract has conferred upon them, to avail themselves of the facility which the locality affords them, of using a material that will cost the least. There is every reason, then to suppose that a great portion of the tower will consist of Hoad stone, quarried from the rock to which we have already alluded. Independent of its soft and ragged qualities, it has, when used for building purposes, a very unsightly appearance. The majority of the houses in this part of the country are built of a similar kind, but better stone; hence it is that rough-cast -a cheap substitute for cement -is generally used as a finish to the out-sides , and which also adds to their warmth by keeping them dry. If then it is necessary to take these precautions with common buildings in sheltered situations, how much more necessary is it that the proposed tower should be constructed of materials capable of withstanding the pelting storm, blow from what quarter it may; for a more exposed site than the top of Hoad for a building, it would be difficult to point out. It has been suggested to us, by an experienced mason, that the surface-limestone on Birkrigg would be most suitable for the outside facing, which is well adapted for such a purpose, from its long exposure to the weather. It would require but little dressing; and its natural face would add materially to the grandeur of the structure. The dome should be built of picked limestone, which would also add to its beauty, by its durable whiteness.

The subscriptions at this time, amount to about £900; £525 is the sum for which the contractors have agreed to build the tower, leaving a balance, as the subscriptions at present stand, of £375 for the joiner's work and other etceteras. Now would it not be better to offer the contractors £200 more -a sum which our informant states would pay them well -to build the outside facing of Birkrigg limestone; and thus secure a strong and handsome building, a building that would last for centuries -than to have one run up of soft and unsightly material, one that will never be finished, because it will never be dry, and always under repair?

One great objection to Hoad stone is, that it cannot be got in sufficiently large blocks to make a firm and solid wall. While under the process of dressing, it rives into flakes and requires bedding with the smaller portions or refuse.

If the plan, as at present laid down, be persisted in, we shall have merely a piece of patchwork masonry to gaze at, while on the other hand, an outside facing of Birkrigg Limestone, would give to the tower a bold and massive appearance which would be in strict keeping with the nature of the scenery by which it would be surrounded.

In the latter case many of the subscribers would, we have no doubt, increase the amount of their subscriptions; indeed several have already offered to do so, and one gentleman who has taken a lively interest in the matter, has promised to increase his subscription ten guineas, provided the tower is built of limestone. We hope, therefore, that steps will be taken to make the building worthy of the object for which it is intended.

18th April 1850
The Hill of Hoad.
Woodburn Postlethwaite, Esq., of Hoad Cottage, has within the last few weeks, set an example to the Ulverstonians, which we hope to see followed with suitable spirit and liberality in the autumn of the present year. We allude to the planting with ornamental trees, at that gentleman's private expense, each side of the principal entrance to Hoad. Those of our readers who value the beautiful and unrivalled walks, that wind over, and around the hill, either for their health's sake, or the love of nature, surely will

not grudge a few shillings, bestowed for the purpose of ornamenting the walks, and seats, and craggy rocks, of this favourite haunt of both sexes; -where youth is ever delighted to ramble without restraint, and old age is fain to climb, slowly though it be, even with the aid of the staff and the crutch.

The neighbourhood of Ulverston has very many beautiful spots, and not a few enchanting walks and rambles, but there is nothing like Hoad. Let a few pounds be judiciously laid out in planting trees and shrubs, and in other ornamental improvements, and the hill of Hoad cannot fail to become one of the chief attractions of the lake district, crowned as it will be, ere long, with that proud memorial of individual worth and greatness, the Barrow Monument.

Correspondent.

2nd May 1850

THE LIMESTONE OF FURNESS. BARROW MONUMENT..

To the Editor of the *Ulverston Advertiser*. Sir.- I have often thought how strange it is that men may live and move for years amid objects of great intrinsic value and importance, without being conscious of these objects being either important or valuable. Strange is it too, to notice how eagerly men will send for objects from a considerable distance and pay a high price for them, on account of their real or imaginary celebrity, when they have at hand the same or similar objects equally valuable, if not more so, and obtainable at a much less cost. I have been led into these general remarks from a consideration of the fact that the *limestone of Furness* is so little appreciated, as a first-class building material, in this district, and almost utterly unknown to the world. I do not, however, despair of our valuable marble becoming in after years, as celebrated as it is now unknown; and to aid in making known its value, we must invoke the mighty ---- of the press. It has been the case in all ages of the world, both with regard to inventions and the wondrous productions of nature, that they have been despised and contaminated for many years. -Sometimes a people rising to destroy us was the case with the machine *a-la-Jacauard*. In France*,* what afterwards they have idolised as an instrumentality of national greatness.

I have seen and carefully examined, both in the quarry and in buildings, most of what are ruled the finest stones in the kingdom- such as *Derbyshire and Kendal Marbles and the Portland, Bath, and Rocks Abbey-----stones*, but I feel convinced that in point of *durability* and *utility*, our limestone is *fully equal* to, and in point of *beauty of colour* it surpasses the whole of those I have mentioned. And yet, when we look at our great limestone storehouses at Birkrigg, Urswick, Hawkfield, Stainton, Gleaston Castle, Dunnerholme, Plumpton, Baycliffe, &c, &c, the quantity taken away, though some of the quarries have been open for a century or more, compared with the almost inexhaustible treasures, seems only as if some geologist had been chipping off a few pocket specimens. Surely, sir, we cannot suppose but that Providence in up-heaving these mighty masses of mountain- limestone, amid and around our celebrated primitive rocks, has done so for wise and beneficent purposes. Within the circuit of a few miles -within the easy glance of the eye, we have our slate quarries from the primitive rocks - our iron ores, our copper ores - our carboniferous limestone, our magnesium limestone, and our new red sandstone, and doubtless we have also coal. But I must return from this digression.

The question then arises what is the best mode of displaying the beauty of this valuable marble – this California of Furness? I answer, we have at this present moment, a most suitable opportunity of doing so in the erection of the *Barrow Monument;* the plan of which as designed by the eminent architect employed, Mr. Trimen, is all that could be desired, *provided it is built in the best possible manner.* There is, however, reason to fear that such will not be the case, unless great efforts are made in Ulverston to raise subscriptions. The fear that I have is, that the building will be a RUBBLE WALL. If so, it is impossible to display the character of our limestone in such a style of building; nor will the Monument be so chaste and beautiful as it is so desirable it should, and as it would be if it were built in ashlar. Shall we let the golden opportunity pass, of aiding in doing honour to departed worth and excellence, and at the same time, shewing one of the treasures of this beautiful locality. I cannot think so meanly of the public spirit of the town. It is not yet too late to remedy the evil; but if the matter is to be done, then it were well it were done quickly. Your paper has already recorded one most liberal promise of increased subscription if the Monument is built in ashlar; and I have heard several express their willingness to subscribe according to their means, if the matter is set about in right good earnest.

I would suggest, therefore, the propriety of calling a town's meeting, and invite the attendance of all classes, and organize an effective working local committee to collect subscriptions from ten pounds or more, down to sixpence from the poorest man in town, and co-operate with the committee in London. There is everything in the object contemplated, calculated to arouse our best, our most enthusiastic exertions. It is to do honour to a townsman, who was an honour to the town, and one who did the "state some service." The committee in London has conferred a great honour on Ulverston, in selecting Hoad as the best site for the Monument, and it becomes us to show ourselves worthy of the honour, and that we appreciate it not only heartily in the abstract, but palpably by getting a long subscription list. I feel convinced that the matter needs but commencing; and who so likely to take the initiative as those who have here so liberally subscribed and taken an active part in the matter? Let them call a public meeting, and I feel sure they will be supported in a manner worthy of the town and the occasion. Let the relatives of Sir John and the distinguished friends who are purposing to honour the laying the foundation-stone with their presence, have the high gratification of knowing before they come, that Ulverston has nobly done its duty -has indeed surpassed itself in liberality; and that the Monument will, in its workmanship, be more beautiful, more finished, more classical, than the funds at present at the disposal of the committee justify them in contemplating, BY THE PUBLIC SPIRIT, THE PROMPT AND ADEQUATE LIBERALITY OF THE GOOD OLD TOWN. Such a fact cannot fail to give zest to the interesting proceedings so near at hand, and the building when so completed will shew that we have a beautiful marble capable of being wrought in a style, that cannot fail to command the admiration of every visitor -and our limestone will become more known and appreciated throughout the kingdom. J. B.

9th May 1850
We extract the following paragraph on the above subject from the *Morning Herald* of Tuesday: -"The ceremony of laying the first stone of the testimonial to the late Sir John Barrow, Bart, is intended to take place at Ulverston, on Wednesday, the 15th of May, on which occasion Sir George Barrow, Bart, (accompanied by his brother, Mr. Barrow, of the Admiralty) is expected to attend, for the purpose. We are glad to find that the subscriptions to the testimonial already amount to upwards of £1,000/, and to notice, among the more recent subscribers, several additional names of the nobility and gentry:- the Duke of Beaufort, 5/-.; the Earl of Lonsdale, 5/-.; Sir James Graham, £10-10s; the Earl of Ripon, 5/-.; the Marquis Camden, 5/-.; Viscount Palmerston, 5/-.; &c. The design selected by the committee is that of Mr. Andrew Trimen, architect, whose elaborate work on Church and Chapel Architecture, together with an account of the Hebrew Church, may be known to some of our readers. The stone tower designed by him is to be 100 feet in height, by 40 feet diameter at the base; and as this structure is to be erected on the Hill of Hoad, which rises immediately above the town of Ulverston, to the height of 450 feet, the effect will be striking. The tower will serve as a sea mark for the navigation of the dangerous bay of Morecambe, and will also, in all probability, be the means of saving the lives of many persons in crossing the sands at Ulverston. Preparations, we understand, to a great extent are in progress at Ulverston, every one, from the highest to the lowest, being anxious to vie with his neighbour in showing their respect to the memory of their distinguished townsman."

16th May 1850
Laying of the Foundation Stone.
The ceremony of laying the Foundation Stone of the Barrow Monument on the summit of the Hill of Hoad, which has been for some time the absorbing theme of interest to the inhabitants of this town and neighbourhood, took place yesterday. The weather which of late had been distinguished for a sunny sky, though with the somewhat harsh and ungenial winds for the "sweet month of May," on Monday evening suddenly assumed a showery character.

Tuesday was marked by showers and sunshine alternatively, till towards evening, but the night throughout proved fair and fine, and the morning sun of yesterday rose resplendently.

At an early hour the bells of St. Mary's Church sent forth glad peals, and the Ulverston brass band gave inspiring and joyous strains from the Market-place, arousing the people to the coming events of the day. The Town Bank School, associated as it ever must be with the early life of the distinguished individual whose memory to future ages was about to be perpetuated, presented a gay appearance; -wreathed in evergreen with the proud Flag of England, sent from the Admiralty office for the occasion, waving over its roof, and streamers floating in the breeze stretching from the belfry to the eminence in the field adjoining, appeared glorying, as it were, in the once humble scholar it had sent forth upon the world to gather, in the paths of industry and science, reputation and renown. At the foot of the bank, a triumphal arch, decorated with several greens and flags had been erected, displaying the very trite motto
"Be his the palm that merits it."

Over which was placed the Arms of the Barrow Family. Within a few yards, but of smaller dimensions, another was placed over the gateway of the occupation road, leading to Hoad, bearing the motto,
"Virtue survives the grave."

Flags also were seen flying on the site of the Monument-on the steeple of St. Mary's Church,-on the vessels in the port,- upon the straw-roofed cot in which the late Baronet first saw light of a world in which he was destined to enact so distinguished a part. Indeed, King Street, Market Street, Upper Brook Street &c., appeared one continuous display of Flags, Banners, and Mottoes evincing clearly and indisputably, that a great amount of taste and industry had been bestowed upon them by the fair labourers of Ulverston. Various other places were also similarly decorated, but our space forbids us further to enumerate, except to mention that a very handsome arch of evergreens was suspended over the street from Mr. Atkinson's to Mr. Turner's shop, and another at the top of Soutergate.

The town, indeed, as early as eight o' clock, presented, altogether, an animated appearance; some hundreds of the inhabitants might then be seen congregated in groups in every quarter; and which as the day advanced, were swelled by thousands more, who flocked in from the surrounding neighbourhood, to wait the formation of the procession.

It began to move at about one o' clock under the direction of Sergeant Major Bates, (W.) of the Duke of Lancaster's Own Yeomanry Cavalry, in the following order:
Superintendent Davidson, and the members of the Ulverston Constabulary.
The Ulverston Brass Band.
The Pensioners, Naval and Military.
The Members of the various Friendly Societies of the Town, with the Flags, Banners, and Emblems of the different Orders, arranged according to seniority, viz:-
The Union Friendly Society.
The Morecambe Lodge of the Independent Order of Oddfellows.
The Lightburne Star Lodge (branch) of the Independent Order of Oddfellows.
The Furness Star Lodge of the grand United Order of Oddfellows.
The Friendship, Love and Truth Lodge (branch) of the Grand United Order of Oddfellows.
The Band of the Messrs. Salmon.
The Scholar's of the Public Schools, arranged also according to seniority headed by their Masters and Teachers, as follows; -
The Town Bank Scholars (day).
The Town Bank Scholars (Sunday).
The National Scholars (day).
The National Scholars (Sunday).
The Wesleyan Scholars (Sunday).

The Independent Chapel Scholars (Sunday).
The Roman Catholic Scholars (day & Sunday).
The Ulverston Union Workhouse Scholars.
The Regimental Band of the 52nd Light Infantry.
Sir George Barrow & Mr. John Barrow and friends, accompanied by the Committee and Subscribers.
Mr. Trimen, the Architect.
Mr. Smith, Contractor for the Works.
Messrs. Brocklebank, bearing Trowel and Level.
The Clergy, Magistrates, and Inhabitants of the Town and neighbourhood.

In this order the procession began to move at one o' clock, proceeding from the Market place through King-street, up Soutergate, by the Town Bank School, where it halted, whilst the following Verses, written by Miss Agnes Strickland, for the occasion, (a lively incentive to the elder scholars to act well the part allotted them,) was sung by the children of the Infant School;-

We'll sing the Town Bank Scholar,
Who once was poor as we,
 And won his way by merit
 To wealth and high degree.

Three cheers for Noble Barrow,
Ye Town Bank Scholars raise,
He was your elder Brother,
And well deserves your praise.

Three cheers again and louder,
Till Cartmel crags reply,
Old Torver from his mountain throne,
Shall echo back our cry.

The Dalesman all shall listen,
And look to Hoad's green height,
While ancient school mates of the Bank
His story shall recite.

And praise the generous spirit,
Of him, who ne'er forgot,
Midst proudest scenes of splendour
Old Dragley's lowly cot.

Now three times three for Barrow,
The glory of our Town;
And long may this Memorial
His native mountain crown.

We'll make him our example
For those who strive to gain,
By noble means, distinction,
Will never strive in vain.

At the conclusion of which the procession proceeded by Mr. Bates' Summer House, to the site of the Monument where it arrived about two. The procession having taken ground under the direction of Mr. Bates, and so placed as to give a circular and uninterrupted area round the base of the Monument, and the police, assisted by the members of the Friendly Societies appointed to keep the same from being unhinged upon, the ceremony commenced by the children singing a Hymn, written for the occasion by Mr. John Stanyan Biggs and set to music by Mr. R. Daniel, organist of the parish church. Respecting this Hymn we may mention here, that it had been the intention of the Committee in London, to request the late lamented Poet Laureate to furnish a composition of a similar character, but his unexpected illness and death prevented the accomplishment of the task. Mr. J. S. Bigg was then applied to and supplied the following:-

> Lord of all light, and life, and love.
> Lord of all majesty, and power,
> Whose brightness shines in every star,
> Whose goodness breathes to every flower;
> Amid the splendour of thy co---it,
> The-----luster of thy train.
> Look on thy----worshippers,

And hear the---- of their strain;
To thee be adoration given.
Thee in the highest, -King of Heaven;

Still, amid the lightning-glitterings,
That --- --- --- --- angels ---,
--- --- --- --- ---
--- --- --- --- ---
Lord Hallelujah to thy praise,
Thine --- --- the --- ---
Of --- --- --- ---
And --- --- --- on the ---
The --- --- --- of ---
To thee be adoration given,
Thee in the highest, - King of Heaven!

We praise thee O!
For all the love and --- --- ---
To one whose heart--- --- ---
In mute thanksgiving to thy throne;
One whose meek spirit was endow'd
With all the grace to virtue given,
The peace, the joy, the blessedness,
And the sweet hope that comes from heaven:
To thee be adoration given,
Thee in the highest – King of Heaven!

The ev'ning of a life well spent,
Drew on --- --- tranquil, alone,
The shadows lengthen'd, till at last,
Death, like a slumber, brought repose,
And he is gone, - gone to a world,
--- and holier far than this,
A world whose monarch is our God,
And the soul's portion – endless bliss.
To thee be adoration given,
Thee in the highest, – King of Heaven.

(We submit also here an extract from the Auto-Biography of Sir John Barrow, Bart., showing that through his instrumentality, Sunday schools were first established in Ulverston.)

"All my old school fellows had long ago departed this life. My little property has equally, long since, been disposed of. The younger and surviving branches of the family never knew me, and all that keeps up the recollection of the townspeople, are a few Charities, with which my name, and others of my family here are associated; and of which there is one in particular I have reason to be proud of,- the establishment of a Sunday School. Just after leaving school, in a conversation with a young friend, we lamented that there was no such thing as a Sunday School, for the benefit of poor Children. I suggested that we should prepare one, but how? There was no newspaper, not even a printing press. We, however, drew up a plan, and I undertook to stick it up on the market cross, the night before market day. We saw that it excited great attention; it was talked of; a person offered himself to undertake it, and it succeeded so well, that to the Ulverstone Sunday School, I and some of my family are at this time Annual Subscribers."

Mr. Smith, the builder, in a brief address, presented a beautifully wrought silver trowel with ivory handle, to Sir George Barrow, together with a bottle containing the several current coins of the realm, viz, -Half-farthing, Farthing, Half-penny, Penny, Fourpenny, Sixpenny, Shilling. Florin, Half-a-Crown, Crown, Half-a-Sovereign and Sovereign. Also a copy of the *Ulverston Advertiser* : which having been deposited, by the son of Sir George Barrow, in the cavity prepared for its reception, -

SIR GEORGE BARROW said- The bottle now placed in that cavity contains the current coin of the realm, so that after many hundreds of years, should it be opened, it will be discovered in what reign this monument was erected. (Cheers.) I will now proceed to lay the foundation stone, (which he then did, assisted by his brother, Mr. John Barrow, amid the loud cheering of the assembled multitude.)

The stone with the following inscription having been lowered, received several strokes from the mallet, (one prepared for the occasion, wrought in mahogany,) and Sir George Barrow's son having applied the level, a mahogany instrument, to the stone. Sir George Barrow declared the stone properly laid.

> ON THE 16TH MAY, A.D. 1850,
> IN THE 14TH YEAR OF THE REIGN OF
> HER MOST GRACIOUS MAJESTY, QUEEN VICTORIA,
> SIR GEORGE BARROW, BART.,
> AND JOHN BARROW, ESQ, F.R.S.
> DEPOSITED THIS STONE TO RECORD THE
> COMMEMORATION OF THE
> TESTIMONIAL TO THE LATE SIR JOHN BARROW, BART.
> ANDREW TRIMEN, ARCHITECT.

Three times three cheers were then called for which were given in a most enthusiastic manner.

Sir George Barrow then said – My esteemed friends, I had almost said my fellow townsmen, from the hearty reception I have met with. This is a memorable day for Ulverston; I am here not to assist in raising a family monument only, though I hope that in the duty I am performing, I am obeying one of God's commandments, the first with promise, in honoring my Father, but I am here, on the part of the noblemen and gentlemen of England who are subscribers to the monument, to lay the foundation of a testimonial , to record the high sense they entertain of the public worth of your revered townsmen and my beloved parent. It is with just pride and real gratitude that I find myself called upon to take so prominent a part in this interesting ceremony, and the more so, as I am assured that you are content that the immediate descendant of your honored townsman should hold that position which might have been confirmed on some eminent person. I rejoice to think that the departed worth of one who was born here, will now be brought home as it were to your daily memories by the erection of this memorial, and I fervently trust that it may continue for ages an ornament to this beautiful district, a place of resort for its inhabitants, and for strangers, where many a tribute of respect will be paid; a beacon for the shipping of the bay, and an encouraging token for the guidance of the rising generation in the paths which lead to honor and renown. My kind friend and your excellent pastor will pray for a blessing on this undertaking, but I will offer one petition to the Author of all good, in which I am sure you will join.

"O Lord prosper Thou our work upon us,
Prosper Thou our handy work."

The Rev. R. Gwillym made prayer as follows:-

O Lord God Almighty, the Creator, Preserver, and Upholder of all things, both in Heaven, and in Earth, without whose blessing and protection nothing is strong, nothing can prosper, look down, we beseech Thee, with thy favour on the work, we are here assembled to undertake. In no spirit of vain boasting do we lay the foundation stone of this memorial, in no feeling of pride or presumption shall we proceed with the superstructure. We desire by it to perpetuate the name of one, to whom Thou wast pleased to grant a long and prosperous life, and whom by thy grace Thou didst enable to do his duty faithfully and energetically amidst the varied and eventful scenes, through which he passed. We freely confess, we can neither think, nor do anything, that is rightful without Thee-to Thee therefore do we give all the praise of any worthy actions, which thy servant performed, we bless Thee for so ordering his steps that he was permitted to exhibit an example worthy of imitation in the fidelity and diligence, sincerity and devotion, with which he discharged this duty to his Sovereign and Country, during many years of active and arduous public service, in various climes, and under trying circumstances. Grant that the honourable name which by thy blessing he acquired, by the same blessing may prove the means of inciting others to pursue a like beneficial career.

More especially we commend to thy favour and benediction the young persons here present, let thy fatherly hand ever be over them, let thy Holy Spirit ever be with them, and so lead them in the knowledge and obedience of Thy Word, that they may adorn the doctrine of God their Saviour in all things, and be useful members of the community, to which they belong. Let this be no empty Ceremonial, rather let it speak to them a stirring lesson, inculcating the duties of their respective conditions, and inspiring them with an earnest desire to perform all that is due from them. While they look on the scene before them, teach them in humble dependence on Thee, and with devout prayers for thy aid to resolve, that they will lead no idle and unprofitable life, but will seek thy honour and glory above all things, and strive to deserve well of their fellow men by devoting the best energies of their minds and bodies to promote the general good.

Implant in their hearts, we entreat Thee, such principles of sound morality and pure religion that they may become loyal and dutiful subjects of our beloved Queen, true lovers of their Country, and above all, faithful and obedient servants of the Lord Jesus Christ.

Finally, we implore the continuance of those manifold and great blessings, both temporal and spiritual, which Thou hast bestowed on the Land of our Birth. Let Thine Almighty Arm be extended over us for our protection. Let thy wisdom guide and defend our Gracious Sovereign Lady, Queen Victoria; direct and prosper the counsels and endeavours of those who are put in authority under Her, that in all things they may seek to promote thy glory, and the welfare of mankind; let justice and holiness, let peace and love, with all the virtues which adorn the Christian profession, flourish and abound among us now and for ever more. May all orders and degrees of men in their---- and ministry truly and----serve Thee and---in constant-----for the------direction of Thy---spirit, and in praising Thee for Thy great and undeserved mercies towards us.

Accept we beseech Thee O Heavenly Father---- our imperfect prayers and------------------ Amen.

Prevent us O Lord, in all our doings, with thy most gracious favour, and further us with thy continual help; that in all our works, begun, continued, and ended in these, we may glorify thy

holy Name and finally by thy mercy obtain everlasting life; through Jesus Christ our Lord. Amen.
Lord's Prayer.
Benediction.

Soon after the devotional part of the ceremony was concluded three times three were given for Lady Barrow.

Sir George Barrow. In acknowledging the compliment, said -On behalf of my wife I thank you most sincerely. I am sure this day can never be forgotten by either of us. I trust the work may go on and prosper.

Three cheers were then given for Mr. John Barrow, which compliment he briefly acknowledged: after which cheers were given for "The Lancashire Witches;" likewise for "Major Davis."

Major Davis in responding said, -I thank you for the reception which you have given me. The late Sir John Barrow was an able and valuable public servant, and highly respected. He (Sir John Barrow) rose from the position of a poor man, by his own integrity and perseverance, to the high position which he held in the Admiralty. (He then briefly alluded to the travels of Sir John Barrow, and the works which he had published, and urged upon all present to follow his example.)

Sir George Barrow next called for three cheers for the Rev. R Gwillym, which he acknowledged in a very appropriate address.

Major Davis proposed three cheers for the clergy which were given in a most admirable manner. Four verses of the 112th Psalm, were then sung to the music of the 150th by the children.

> That man is blest, who stands in awe
> Of God, and loves his sacred law;
> His seed on earth shall be renown'd,
> And with successive honours crowne'd.

> His house, the seat of wealth, shall be
> An inexhausted treasury;
> His justice, free from all decay.
> Shall blessings to his heirs convey.
>
> The soul that's fill'd with virtue's light
> Shines brightest in affliction's night;
> To pity the distress'd inclin'd;
> As well as just to all mankind.
>
> Beset with threat'ning dangers round,
> Unmov'd shall he maintain his ground
> The sweet remembrance of the just
> Shall flourish when he sleeps in dust.

The ceremony concluded by the Regimental Band playing the National Anthem. This Band, 24 in number, sent forth the most ravishing martial strains, and was certainly one of the great attractions of the day.

Never has the hoary hill that stands on the confines of our little town witnessed an exhibition so imposing as that which the proceedings of yesterday presented. The congregated thousands who had gathered from all quarters to witness the ceremony; the troops of bright eyed children belonging to the various Day and Sunday schools in the town; the members of the different Friendly societies, each bearing their appropriate badges; the banners of the various orders flaunting proudly in the sun shine; the bursts of martial music, that at intervals startled the echoes that slumbered in the surrounding valleys and rural dells; all conspired to bring back tales of half forgotten times, -suggesting broken fragments and affording sunny glimpses of the Past, loosely connected together by an imaginary link of coincidences, till the whole produced a medley series of reminiscences, in which distant times and places seemed strangely intermingled with one another, and with the present. The music and the banners served to suggest the Age of Chivalry, when Martial Knights were ready to peril life and limb for the light of "Ladye's eye", while the singing of the children in honour of the departed, transported us to those times when the Minnesingers and the Meister-singers of Germany, and the light-hearted Troubadors of Provence improvised for the "pleasurance" of their lordly patrons.

The scene itself was singularly in harmony with the reminiscences which the proceedings on the bill were calculated to awaken. To the north, the large form of Coniston Old Man appeared, lifting his pointed peak into the sky; while around him on the other hand, but at a greater distance, the mountains of Westmoreland and Cumberland- a banded brotherhood -stretched their vast proportions over many miles of the distant landscape. Nearer at hand were hills of inferior altitude, between which, like opening vistas into Faery Land, the eye ran up long defiles, catching in its course the smile of many white-washed cottages standing in the midst of pleasant meadows and verdant valleys. To the east, appeared the waters of the Bay of Morecambe, confined between the shores at Greenodd on the one hand, and the Cartmel chain of hills on the other, the opposite shore fringed with trees, -a glorious mirror with a foliated frame; while to the south, the waters of the same bay gleamed over an ampler area, between indented shores, and bordered by luxuriant meadows, like the Queen of beauty with a zone of emeralds, its shining surface reflecting a lustre as unspotted and untarnished as the silver Shield of Oberon. Amidst this lavish magnificence of nature it is only left for us to express a hope that the name of him, whose virtues this day's proceedings were intended to commemorate, may be as firmly established amidst the shifting sands of Time , as are the rocky foundations of the mountain whose summit is destined to be crested with the memorial to his honor.

The procession having re-formed, returned by the western side of the hill, on the serpentine paths recently made, egressing by the gate at Oubas Hill; thence by the Canal-head, Sunderland Terrace, Fountain-street, King-street, and the Market-place, where it took position, and dispersed with regularity and order.

The Friendly Societies were afterwards treated to dinner at their several Lodges, viz:
The Union Friendly, at Mr. Neale's Hope & Anchor Inn. Duke street; the Morecambe Lodge of the Independent Order of Oddfellows, at Mrs.. Worthington's Queen's Arms Inn; and its Branch Society, the Lightburn Lodge, at Mr. Gelderd's the Victory Inn; the Furness Star Lodge of the Grand United Order of Oddfellows, at Mr. Barnett's, the King's Arms Inn; and its Branch Society, the Friendship, Love, and Truth Lodge, at Mr. Postlethwaite's The Commercial Inn. The Children of the Infant School were regaled by their patron, the Rev. R. Gwillym, at his residence, at Stock-bridge; and all the other scholars (with the exception of those of the Workhouse) at the National School, in the Ellers; the Workhouse children, at the expense of B. Gilpin, Esq., partook of dinner at the Braddyll's Arms Inn, previous to setting out of the procession, and at its conclusion after partaking of refreshments at the Workhouse, in the evening, were regaled by the same gentleman, at his cottage at Dragley Beck, and encouraged in a succession of sports in the grounds and meadows there, which were kept up by the party with happy glee till the waning day compelled them to desist. The company assembled on the Hill of Hoad at the above ceremony, were computed by the military gentlemen present at 8,000.

In returning from the ceremony, the procession as it wound round the head of Hoad, formed one of the grandest and most imposing spectacles it has ever been our lot to witness. No description of ours would enable the reader to form a faithful conception it presented, as the serpentine walks became gradually filled, until from the top to the bottom, an apparently endless chain of living links of human machinery appeared to have been set in motion. The effect was heightened by the display of numerous gay coloured flags, which imparted to the whole, the character of a grand romance rather than a scene of reality.

THE DINNER.
At which Sir George Barrow, Bart., his brother, Mr. John. Barrow, F.R.S., Major Davis, and other friends of the family were

entertained in honour of the event, took place at the Athenaeum Assembly Rooms, (the walls of which were tastefully decorated for the occasion,) was supplied by Mr. Smith, of the Sun Inn----when, the style in which it was served up,----the greatest credit c---of every delicacy the season could afford- Turtle, Turbot, Champagne and Punch:- the deserts and wine were excellent, and served up in ample grandness. The band of the 52nd Regiment played at intervals during the evening and enlivened the company by its spirit-stirring strains: about 80 sat down to the tables, among whom were -Sir George Barrow, Bart., and Son John Barrow, Esq., Bernard Gilpin, Esq., (chairman,) Thomas Woodburne, Esq. (vice chairman,) The Revs; R, Gwillym, J. Baldwin, J Macauley, M. Forrest, W. Oliver, W. Dawson, J. Hughes, J. Galkarth, J.G. Morris, Major Davis of the 52nd Light Infantry, James Clarke, Esq., E. D. Salisbury, Esq., G. Sunderland, Esq., R. N., H. Remington, Esq., John Fell, Esq., H. F. Rigge, Esq., W. Ainslie, Esq., F. Ward, Esq., E. J. Schollick, Esq., R. Remington Esq., G. Remington, Esq., J. B. Smith, Esq., W. Yarker, Esq., Wm. Postlethwaite . Esq., Broughton, Sergeant Major Bates, (W.) James Davis Esq., James Davis, Esq., jun, T. Roper, Esq., R. Roper, Esq, jun., S. J Bolleau, Esq., Jonathan Thompson Esq., of Stubbing Court, F. Barratt, Esq., John Cooper, Esq., (Preston), J. Gorman, Esq., Mayor of Preston, A. Trimen, Esq., Architect, Mr. Smith, Contractor for the Works, Capt. J. Barrow, Mr. W. F. D. Dickinson, Mr J. Stanyan Biggs, Mr. Potter, Mr. G. Clominson, Ambleside, and the principle Tradesmen of the town.

The Chairman, Bernard Gilpin, Esq., in proposing the first toast, "The Queen," observed that no good man of Furness would hesitate for a moment in joining in the hearty wish that Her Majesty's reign might be long, happy, prosperous, and peaceful both at home and abroad. (Cheers.)
Band , National Anthem.

The Chairman next gave in succession, "Prince Albert, and the rest of the Royal family."---" The High Sheriff." and the "Lord Lieutenant," which were drunk with hearty cheers. "The Army and Navy" followed, coupled with the name of Major Davis, who acknowledged the high compliment paid to the service in which he had the honour of holding a commission, and alluded to the procession, which he characterised as one of the most orderly and imposing nature. He felt proud to say that whenever he was called upon, and he also felt that he could answer for the whole of his brethren in arms, that his regiment would be found ready to do its duty in defence of the nation whenever required whether at home or abroad. He would leave to his honourable friend, Captain Sunderland, the duty of responding on behalf of the Navy.

Captain Sunderland then rose and expressed his sincere thanks for the complimentary manner in which the latter part of the toast had been received; particularly on an occasion like the one they had met to commemorate; viz, the name of one who had for so lengthened a period so high a position connected with the Navy, and from whom he had himself received much kindness, and for whose memory he entertained the highest respect. He considered that Ulverston had every reason to be proud that it had been selected for the place to immortalise the name of Sir John Barrow; and concluded by wishing prosperity to his descendants. (Cheers) Band—"British Grenadiers," and "Rule Britannia."

The Chairman then in an appropriate address, proposed "The Lord Bishop of the Diocese and the Clergy."

The Rev. R. Gwillym responded.- He said, they had drunk the health of the "Army and Navy," and now they were drinking the health of the Army at home, which he trusted would be encouraged, that they might go onwards. We must not, he continued, look at those who lived in former times, but endeavour to advance in the knowledge of all that was good. It had been his good fortune, since he had come amongst them, to receive much kindness from his parishioners. He had been now nearly sixteen years amongst them, and he trusted the same good feeling would prevail in their breasts towards him so long as it pleased the Almighty to permit him to exercise over them his spiritual care.

The Rev. J. Baldwin, on being called upon by the chairman, as being an intimate friend of the Bishop's, briefly alluded to his visit amongst them last summer.

Major Davis then rose to propose the toast of the evening. "The memory of the late Sir John Barrow, Bart.," in proposing which he felt a great personal gratification, the late Baronet having been an intimate friend of his own, as were also, he was happy to say, the whole of the family, and had been so for many years; indeed he might say from his childhood. He felt it not only a gratifying, but a painful duty in standing before them to propose the toast, which he begged they would drink in solemn silence. Previous however to doing so, he would give them a short history of his late friends' career, as he thought many would wish to know something about it. He would do so to show, that by steady perseverance, and by a man's conduct himself, so as to be a benefit to himself and to his country, that by obtaining knowledge – and knowledge was power – a man might rise to the greatest dignity. (The gallant Major here traced the late Baronet's career from the time he left the town of Ulverston, to the period at which he succeeded to the post at the Admiralty, a situation which he held up to a short season before his death.)

Major Davis, amid loud cheering, proposed "the health of Sir George Barrow," and referred to the proceedings of that day, and the monument that was about to be erected in commemoration of the late Baronet, his father, the design of which was most beautiful, and reflected great credit on the Architect Andrew Trimen, Esq. [A model of the monument was here exhibited to the company, the members of which expressed their admiration of the design.]

The toast was drunk with three times three and one cheer more, the band playing "Auld lang syne."

Sir George Barrow, in acknowledging the toast felt deeply sensible of the great honour conferred upon him. But at the same time he could not but feel that the attention and kindness he had received were shewn to him from the recollection of his dear father. Not that he felt the less proud of the honor they had done him, still he did not wish them to believe that he was vain glorious. It was the happiest day of his life -a day he could never forget, and he would assure them that he should ever feel the greatest interest in the welfare of this district, as did his father, their townsman, though he was never able to visit it; a fact which Sir George accounted for by stating, that during the forty years of his service at the Admiralty, the short time permitted him for relaxation precluded him for so doing. He then alluded to the year in which the Chairman celebrated his father's birth-day at Dragley Beck, a mark of esteem which was not only deeply and gratefully appreciated by the deceased Baronet, but by all the members of his family. He once more repeated, that he felt himself unable to convey to the company present, the intense interest which the proceedings of the day had raised in his breast, and the sense he entertained of the honour which had been done him, by all whom he had the pleasure of meeting. (Cheers.)

The Chairman, in terms highly eulogistic of the services performed by the gallant 52nd and stating at the same time, that he would introduce to the notice of the company, an old pensioner belonging to the same regiment, and who had fought in six out of the following battles in which the corps had been engaged, viz:- Hindoostan-Vimiera-Corunna-Busaco-Fuentes D'onor- Cludad Rodrigo-Badajoz-Salanianca-Vittoria-Nivelle-Nive- Orthes-Toulouse-Peninsula-Waterloo:-proposed "the health of Major Davis and the gallant 52nd" and was confident if they should be engaged in any action hereafter, they would distinguish themselves as they had done in the days of yore. (Cheers.)

Major Davis expressed his thanks for the warm and handsome manner in which the toast had been received; and alluded in flattering terms to the old pensioner (who had entered the room,) and hoped if their services should be required, they would distinguish themselves as they had hitherto done. He concluded by stating that he had felt great pleasure in having the good fortune to take part in the day's proceedings, and that he would at all times be ready to lend them his aid upon any occasion of a similar nature.

Sir George Barrow, in proposing the health of the worthy president of the evening, dwelt upon the highly satisfactory manner in which that gentleman had discharged the onerous duties of his office. – Drunk with three times three.

In reply, the Chairman, briefly and humorously acknowledged the compliment that had been paid him, and concluded by observing that his motto was
"Diotis Factisque Simplex."
and whenever he forgot to act up to it, he begged they would forgive him.

The Rev. J. Baldwin gave the health of John Barrow, Esq., F.R.S., upon whom, it was perhaps, not generally known, the mantle of his father had descended; in corroboration of which the reverend gentleman alluded to his literary attainments and enumerated his various works;- "Excursions in the North of Europe," "Tour in Australian Lombardy," "Tour round Ireland," and "Visit to Iceland."

Mr Barrow briefly expressed his acknowledgement of the honor done him, and his gratification with the ceremony of the day, and in conclusion proposed, "the Trustees and Lessee, Woodburne Postlethwaite, Esq., of the town lands" to all whom they were all greatly indebted.

"Sir G. Staunton, the London Committee, and the absent subscribers" was then given by the Chairman, and replied to by Sir George Barrow, who alluded to the services of Captain Beecher, R.N., to whom he said the greatest praise was due for the kind and able manner in which he had conducted the whole of the testimonial to its speedy conclusion. He felt gratified that Ulverston had been selected as the place where the tribute of respect to their fellow-townsmen was to be erected. (Cheers.)

The remains of Sir John Barrow's parents' headstone in the graveyard of the Parish church in Ulverston.

The Monument viewed from Hart Street with Ulverston Victoria School in the foreground. Early 1900's.

View of the Monument from the Entrance to Hoad Hill. Early 1900's.

Nevinson Tradesmen Association parade float, circa 1900.

Bonfire for Queen Victoria's Diamond Jubilee 1897. The fire is made up of brushwood and tar barrels from the local chemical works.

In 1969, due to external structural defects, the Monument was encased in reinforced conctrete at a cost of £7,000. The money was raised by public subscription. Once again, many people climbed the Hoad Hill for the re-opening.

The Chairman said, associated as his mind must be, from early recollections, with the town of Preston, and there being present among them, a gentleman who held the highest municipal office of that Borough, with the company's permission he would propose his health. He then named T. German, Esq.; who in responding expressed the great pleasure he felt in being among them to do honor to departed worth. He was there unprepared to address them at any particular length, but this he would say, that the inhabitants of Ulverston had every reason to be proud of the honor which had been done them; the scene which he had witnessed that day was fraught with interest of the noblest character, especially to the mind of a young man like himself, just entering upon life. They had that day laid the foundation stone of a monument to be erected to their distinguished townsman, who not only obtained the favour of his sovereign, but also the favour of the British nation, and likewise the favour of his fellow-townsmen. He raised himself to the high position which he occupied, by his own individual exertions, and the monument-the foundation stone of which they had that day laid, would not only when completed record his memory, but would point as a beacon to travellers ploughing the briny ocean, by serving as a land mark; and it would also point a magnificent moral to the inhabitants of Ulverston. After a few more remarks upon the benefit likely to accrue to Ulverston from the erection of the monument, he congratulated the committee upon the talented architect which they had chosen, and concluded by proposing "the Town and Trade of Ulverston."

Drunk with acclamation.

Mr. Henry Dickinson, in a neat speech, acknowledged the toast.
The Rev. R. Gwillym remarked that a great omission had been committed in not proposing before "The health of Lady Barrow," who he might state had promised him that she would, accompanied by Sir George Barrow, visit them again on the completion of the monument. Loud Cheer.

Sir George in returning thanks on be half of his Lady, observed that he should feel great pleasure in accepting the kind invitation he and Lady Barrow had received from the Rev. Mr. Gwillym, to become his guest on the occasion named. He then proposed "The health of A. Trimen, Esq., architect."

Mr. Trimen, in a short, but appropriate speech, returned thanks.
J. Cooper Esq., of Preston, was then called upon to propose the health of those men who had fought and bled for their country; who, in complying with the wish, said that he was proud to say, that they had in the country, men who had done the county good service; and after alluding to the service of the 52nd Regiment, and to the great self-reliance displayed by the late Sir John Barrow, he concluded by giving "The Pensioners, Naval and Military." (Cheers.)

"The health of the Vice-President," T. Woodburne, Esq., was next proposed by Sir George Barrow, which that gentleman acknowledged in appropriate terms.

The Rev. J. Hughes gave "The health of Miss Agnes Strickland," and referred to the Hymn which she had written expressly to be sung by the infant children, in that day's ceremony, and the celebrity which she had attained. Cheers.

Mr. John Barrow proposed "The Lancashire Witches," which was received with due honours.

Major Davis proposed "The Lancashire Yeomanry Cavalry." And spoke of their efficiency in the highest terms of praise. Cheers.

Sergeant-Major Bates, on behalf of the officers and men, received the compliment of the gallant Major as highly satisfactory, and trusted the same efficiency would preserve. He availed himself of that opportunity to return thanks on behalf of the Pensioners of Ulverston, and to thank the Chairman for former entertainments which he had given them, and also for the treat which they had received from Sir George Barrow. He then spoke of the kindness of Mr. Cooper to the Pensioners at Preston, whose liberality to them was well know and appreciated throughout the country.

"The health of Mr. H. Remington. Esq.," was then proposed by Sir George Barrow, to whom, he observed, they were greatly obliged for the services he had rendered that day, as a member of the committee of management.

Mr. Remington briefly acknowledged the compliment.

Sir George Barrow next proposed "the health of Mr. Stephen Soulby," who having duly responded to it,

"The health of Mr. J. Stanyan Biggs" was next given by Sir George, amid loud applause.

Mr. J.S. Biggs, in reply said -Gentlemen, I beg to thank you most sincerely for the kind and hearty manner in which you have responded to the toast which has just been proposed. I can assure you that it affords me great satisfaction to have my name brought forward, and received in such a manner as it has been received, upon an occasion like the present, and amidst an assemblage of my own fellow-townsmen. There are few things in this world that contribute more to a man's self-complacency, and which suffice to establish him in that good opinion which every man, is, after all times ready to entertain of himself, than the good opinion of those by whom he is surrounded; and as you have been pleased to testify to me, this evening, the good opinion entertained of me in no equivocal manner, I assure you that it has tended to elevate me in my own self-esteem to no inconsiderable extent. I trust, however, that it may have a more practical as well as a more beneficial tendency in stirring me onward with renewed diligence so that at some future time I may be more worthy of the compliment which has just been paid to me. (Cheers.)

We cannot close our report without bearing our humble testimony to the excellent performances of the 52nd band; whose enlivening and most appropriate airs throughout the evening, afforded the company a great treat. It has seldom been our fortune to listen to music more effectively and pleasingly performed; and in speaking thus our opinion, we are sure that we are only expressing the opinions of all those who were present on the occasion.

THE BARROW MONUMENT
We have received from the best authority, and think it is but justice to the contractors, Messrs. Smith and Appleford, of the firm so long connected with the Admiralty, to remark that they that the have undertaken the whole of the works at an amount that cannot cover the actual costs. This arises from no want of judgement on their part, but simply from their desire to relieve the anxiety of the committee and subscribers, that the expense of the monument shall not exceed the amount set apart from the funds for its erection, viz; -£800, which also includes the expense of the Architect, A Trimen. Esq. Our readers will therefore see from this statement, that the firm above mentioned, stand in the position of a guarantee. The amount of Messrs. Brocklebank's contract as we have before stated, is £535, exclusive of the work and materials employed on the foundation, which has already cost £100, which is to be paid by these gentlemen, who have further agreed to furnish the monument with nearly every requisite in furniture, so that on the closest calculation they will be losers of at least £50; for not less than £225 we are assured will cover the joiners' and iron work. In our next week's impression, we hope, through the kindness of the architect, A. Trimen, Esq., to have the gratification of presenting to our readers an engraving of the Monument as it will appear when finished.

30th May 1850
Shall we then suffer this monument to be built of inferior stone, and in an inferior style of workmanship, when an additional £200 would make it all we could desire. It is impossible to look at the new Bank, to which I referred in my second letter, without desiring that the monument should be built of the same kind of stone; of course we do not expect it to be done in a style like the bank, but feel convinced that, if it is not built in ashlar, with all the other appliances which can give *stability* to the structure, (and

which *its exposed situation so much requires*), we shall all wish it had been so executed, when we see it finished in an inferior style. For it must be remembered that the monument is not like a private dwelling-house, which might never be observed by the passer by, or the stranger, but "like a city set on a hill," which ever way our town is approached the tower will be seen, and when visited, I fear the predominant feeling in every intelligent mind will be that of disappointment. Interesting propositions have been mooted with respect to the interior of the monument, such as a telescope for observation, &c. &c. These objects I cordially approve of, but just now it is most desirable that our *undivided attention* should be directed to the outside of the monument, for depend upon it, if the outside is made an ornament to the town, there will be no lack of funds to complete the inside afterwards.
Yours &c., J.B.

27<u>th</u> June 1850
*A Correspondent says:-*In visiting Hoad lately I was delighted to find a most agreeable accommodation for visitors already in progress in connection with the Monument. I allude to the beautiful limestone seat now in course of erection round the base of the tower. If visitors are fatigued by ascending the hill, here is a delightful seat for their especial use, where they can rest, or repose if they like, and view the surrounding scenery, or dream of its enchanting beauties. They may sit in the sunshine or the shade, in the breeze or in the calm, as their taste, inclinations, or feelings may dictate. The seat is of worked limestone, and bedded and jointed, and the workmanship is most creditable to the builders, and has a most beautiful appearance.

6<u>th</u> February 1851
This beautiful Monument, erected to the Memory of the late Sir John Barrow, Bart., and which had but just been completed, so far as related to its outward form, was on Thursday evening struck by the powerfully vivid lightning, that illumined the country for miles around. The electric fluid, it appears, as stated by Mr. Ainslie, in the course of his Lecture at the Athenaeum, on Tuesday evening - was attracted by the iron girders, and on reaching the lanthorn,

forced its way through the dome, dislodging eight or nine of the massive stones of which it was built. As might have been expected, several of these stones fell inside the building, breaking five out of six of the iron girders, one or two of the landings, and several stone steps; the others falling on the outside, and injuring in their descent, the buttress in two or three different places. The whole of the masonry forming the lanthorn and doom, is also so shaken that those portions will have to be entirely rebuilt. So far, however, as the body of the monument is concerned, it affords us great satisfaction, in being enabled to state, that no trace of damage is discernable. For the information of such of our readers, as have only passed through our district, and particularly for those who have never reached as far as our delightful locality -by the bye, we may as well add, the *healthiest* in England - we do not conceive that it will be out of place, or uncalled for, if we once more transfer to our columns, a description both of the building, and its site.

The Hill of Hoad, on which the Monument – a limestone tower, in the form of a lighthouse, 100 feet high, is erected , - rises immediately above the town of Ulverston, to the height of 435 feet, and was the favourite resort of Sir John in his boyhood. From the summit may be seen the churchyard in which lie buried his, parents – the cottage of his birth at Dragley Beck – and the school at which he was educated. Nor must we omit the grand and beautiful scenery that meets the eye of the visitor at every turn. To the North stands prominently forth Coniston Old Man, and on either side, but at a greater distance, the mountains of the Lakes District. Nearer at hand, between hills of inferior altitude, open to the sight long defiles of verdant valleys. Open to the East appear the waters of the Bay of Morecambe, confined on one side by the shore at Greenodd, and on the other by the Cartmel hills; while to the South the waters of the same Bay gleam over an ample area, between indented shores, bordered by luxuriant meadows, and the Parks of Holker-hall and Conishead Priory. The site of the Tower alone commands, on the Lancaster side, Hestbank, Poulton Ring, Lancaster and the Lune, Fleetwood, and the Wyre, and beyond the geographical limits of the Bay may be seen the entrance to Lytham, Preston, and the Ribble, and in fine weather the mouth of the

Mersey and the Welsh Mountains. The view also commands Piel Harbour, Walney, the entrance to the Duddon, and a portion of the coast and offing seawards, in the direction of Bootle in Cumberland, and as far also as the mountains in the Isle of Man; besides Ingleborough in Yorkshire, and Blackcombe in Cumberland. It will be seen, then, that the site is not only picturesque, but one unsurpassed in magnificence and sublimity.

A singular coincidence, and one worthy of remark, attended the misfortune that has befallen the Tower. The architect, Andrew Trimen, Esq., had forwarded to our office, in the course of the afternoon of the same day, the following letter, which was being perused by us at the moment the flash, (there were but three or four,) which is supposed to be the one that struck the Tower, threw its glare over the town, and sent forth its destructive fluid:-

To the Editor of the Ulverston Advertiser.
Dear Sir.- I think it due to the Contractors for the erection of the above Memorial, to state that, on examination, I have found the whole of the works to be securely and properly built. From the foundation to the top of the dome there is no fissure or opening of the thickness of the paper on which I write; nor, when protected from lightning, can any ever occur; and while this Tower will stand, as stated in the *Nautical Magazine* for the present month, as long as any other in the kingdom, to record an event of general interest, it will at the same time be a Monument to the durability of the stone of Furness, and of the strength of solid masonry.
I am, &c.
"Andrew Trimen, Architect."

The real amount of the damage has not yet been ascertained, but from a rough calculation, we think we may confine it to something under £100. It is much to be regretted that a lightning conductor had not been erected at the completion, of the Monument, but which we understand the want of time only prevented from being carried into effect.

We now must call the attention of our readers, to an advertisement in another part of our paper, (and which will be found a letter, from Commander Beecher, R.N.,) convening a public meeting for Monday next to take into consideration the immediate repair of the tower, and the best means for raising the funds for that purpose. Several gentlemen have already proffered subscriptions towards its restoration, and among the number we may mention, Sir George Barrow, £10; John Barrow, Esq. £25; and Commander Beecher, £5. If we may be permitted to throw out a suggestion, we would advise at the same time, the consideration of a plan for the keeping of the tower, and also a suitable price for admission. It is necessary that something in this way should be done at once. A provision for keeping the Monument in good repair, must be made, and the sooner the better. Of course, whatever plan may be laid down, it will have to receive the satisfaction of the London Committee; but we do not conceive that they can or will take umbrage at any representation made to them emanating from a body of men, who have the perpetration of the memory of Sir John fully at heart. Moreover a fund has yet to be raised for finishing, furnishing, and embellishing the interior, and which alone will prove an inducement for visitors to pay for admission. The London Committee have had, we understand, promised for the tower, a very powerful telescope, which of itself cannot fail to prove a great attraction. Busts of the worthies of the district (Romney for instance for one), to surround that of Sir John, which is now being sculptured by Mr. Young of this town, might also embellish the interior. Nothing in fact ought to be omitted, that will in any way assist to make the BARROW MONUMENT an attractive object to Lake Tourists. Funds for its restoration might be raised, by enlisting those who subscribe half a guinea to a life ticket, one guinea two tickets, and family tickets might also be issued at the same ratio. This, however, as we have before stated is simply a suggestion, which we have taken upon ourselves to throw out for the consideration of the Committee. It is quite certain that the damage must be repaired without delay. Would it not then be advisable, that when that is done, the inside fittings should be commenced? There is little doubt but that the Lake visitors will be greatly increased this summer, by the numbers of foreigners who will be brought to England by the Great Exhibition of Industry. This point we think is one of great importance, and ought not to be lost sight of.

6th February 1851
The Damage Done To THE BARROW TOWER By Lightning
At a Meeting of the subscribers to the Barrow Tower, residents in Ulverston, on Monday the 3rd instant:- "It was unanimously resolved that, a public meeting of the inhabitants of the town and neighbourhood be convened on Monday next, the 10th instant., in the Athenaeum, at 2pm for the purpose of assisting the London Committee with further subscriptions in aid of the restoration of the Tower, which, *at our instance*, they have kindly erected upon Hoad, a Monument so honourable to the memory of our distinguished townsman, so useful to the mariner, to the stranger crossing our pathless and dangerous sands, so ornamental to the landscape, so interesting to ourselves, and hereafter, we hope, to be made still more useful as an Observatory.

Captain Beecher, R. N., Hon. Sec to the London Committee, in reply to the gentleman who communicated the disastrous news to the Admiralty, writes:- "That the Committee, have learnt with deep regret that the Tower just completed in honour of the late Sir John Barrow, on the Hoad Hill, was damaged by lightning on the evening of the 30th ult.; not withstanding directions had been given to the architect to adopt the necessary protection from lightning, so successfully employed by Sir William Snow Harris, and which the want of time only prevented from being carried into effect,"

"Looking at the unfortunate event as one which might have been very much worse in its consequences, the committee are of the opinion that no time should be lost in repairing the damage; and, at the same time, in adopting, as soon as possible, those precautions for security from lightning, that the event has proved to be so imperatively necessary."

"It is with pleasure that the Committee find themselves assisted in carrying out their views by the sum of £36 being placed in their hands for the commencement of a supplementary Subscription List, to which is added the sum of £5 by myself."

6<u>th</u> February 1851
Thursday night, that the earth was not in a positive state, which is frequently the case in winter time; but not during the summer;- that the electricity was attracted by the iron girders which were placed in the building; that the electric fluid passed from one portion of the iron girders to the other, and when it got to the top, there being no more iron the explosion took place and blew out the stones, and it would have blown them out if they had been fifty times as heavy. This was simply the manner in which the accident had occurred; the electric matter having nothing to pass through-no metallic conductors –it became disturbed, and the accident in question was the result; and if a person had been twenty or thirty yards from the tower, most probably he would have felt the shock. Now if the monument had been protected by lightning conductors, there is no doubt this would not have taken place; it, however, he believed, would be protected in that way. He had also been asked, if the monument was thus protected, supposing the town of Ulverston was visited by lightning, whether it would act as a conductor for the property in the town, in answer to which he said he thought not, but that it might serve such a purpose in the immediate vicinity of the tower. It was generally thought that electrical conductors acted as preventives against the effects of lightning to the extent of twice their own distance, and supposing the tower was protected, Hoad standing 400 feet above the level of the sea, and the monument 100 feet in height, making altogether 500 feet, it would consequently only, serve as a protection for the property within the distance of 1000 feet. These were his opinions. Several other experiments next followed, during which he gave an illustration of the galvanic house-guard, and said it was a sure protection against burglars, &c. He concluded his lecture by an experiment of exploding gunpowder under water; remarking that it was impossible to bring before them the whole of the matter and experiments connected with the subject, consequently it had been suggested that Electro-Magnetism should form another lecture, which he should be very happy to give them

when the opportunity permitted. He trusted that as the Athenaeum had been established for instruction and improvement, and as he gave these lectures with the same objects in view, they would have the effect of creating a desire for study in the minds of his young friends and others then present.

The Rev. R. Gwillym then moved a vote of thanks to Mr. Ainslie for his able, instructive, and interesting discourse; which was loudly responded to.

13<u>th</u> February 1851
THE DAMAGE DONE TO THE BARROW TOWER – PUBLIC MEETING. On Monday afternoon last a public meeting (as according to previous announcement) was held in the Assembly-room of the Athenaeum, for "the purpose of assisting the London Committee with further subscriptions in aid of the restoration of the Tower," &c. The Rev. R. Gwillym was unanimously voted to the chair, when it was resolved that a committee should be formed, with the power to add to their number, to divide the town into districts, and to canvas for subscriptions, to repair the damage done to the Tower by lightning. Mr. H. Dickinson was to be requested to act as the treasurer, and Bernard Gilpin Esq., was appointed hon. secretary.

It was stated by the Messrs. Brocklebank, the builders of the Tower, that the cost of repairing the damage which the monument has unfortunately sustained, (full particulars of which we gave in last weeks Advertiser.) would be £140.

It was the unanimous opinion of the meeting that no time should be lost in repairing the damage, and especially when they found themselves assisted in carrying out their views by the sum of £40 being subscribed in London as a commencement of a Supplementary Subscription. The meeting was not numerously attended, but about the sum of £20 was subscribed by the gentlemen present.

13th March 1851
ACCIDENT AT THE BARROW MONUMENT.

On Saturday last, a young man of the name of James Riley, a waller, in the employment of Messrs. Brocklebank , of this town, builders, met with an accident whilst at work in the interior of the Barrow Monument. It will be remembered that in the damage done by the late thunder-storm, the electric fluid in its course had struck the stone steps which were then being erected, some of which at different places in the flight were entirely broken off; and the youth, in descending these steps, fell at one of the broken ones, either from missing his footing or from inadvertence, a height of 45 feet. The consequences of this dreadful fall is that the poor youth has had an arm broken, and is otherwise severely bruised, but we are glad to state that he is progressing as favourably as can be expected. Had he not fallen upon one of the iron girders, about half way down the descent, which intercepted and broke the force of the fall, the result no doubt would have been still more disastrous.

15th May 1851

We copy from the *Morning Herald* of Thursday last, the following notice of the completion of the repairs of this splendid structure.

"The restoration of this beautiful tower, which was struck with lightning in January last, is now nearly completed. Fortunately, the damage sustained was confined to the summit, the main body of the tower having totally escaped injury. It was found necessary to take down the temple which surmounts the tower, and from which several massive stones of three cwt, had been dislodged. The estimated cost of the repair is £120, in consequence of which it is intended to charge an entrance fee to those who may wish to ascend the tower, which would otherwise, we believe, have been thrown open to the public."

We must add that before the charge to the public for entrance can be made consistently, it will be necessary to further the completion of the interior. Not only will it be necessary to erect an iron railing up the stone stairs, but also to lay the flooring of the different stories. Much yet remains to be done before visitors will be induced to ascend to the summit, from whence may be obtained one of the grandest panoramic views in the Lake District, or perhaps in England. It not only behoves the committee, whose object in building the tower, was to perpetuate the memory of a great man, but it is incumbent also on the people of Ulverston and Furness in general, for the character of their district, and their own interests, to exert themselves, to raise the necessary funds for the finishing and decorating the interior. Till this is done, visitors will take but a *passing* view of the monument, and our town will loose the pecuniary benefit, it would otherwise derive.

29th May 1851
To the Editor of the *Ulverston Advertiser*. Sir,-As when the Barrow Monument is made fit for the reception of visitors, there can be no doubt, but that hundreds, yes thousands, will avail themselves of the opportunity of gazing on one of the most beautiful prospects within the Queen's dominions, it becomes a very important question, how can the needful be raised to complete the interior arrangements of the Monument? I mean the stairs, rails, and flooring. I would most earnestly recommend the adoption of the following plan to the London Committee. Let there be issued a series of life tickets (not transferable), on the following scale:- A subscription of :-
Half-a-Guinea - to admit the Subscriber.
One Guinea - to admit a Gentleman and his wife.
Two Guineas - to admit a family of four.
Three Guineas - to admit a family of six.
Five Guineas and upwards to admit a family, governess, and servants, in the charge of children. Suppose £210 were required for fitting up the interior of the Monument, how soon it might be raised if a sufficient number of parties would take tickets. As a matter of health the money would be well laid out. If the inhabitants of Ulverston would ascend Hoad every day, we should not hear so much of nervous affections; nor should we see so many pallid countenances. Let the matter be viewed as a business speculation. If a subscription to the Monument will conduce to the health of self and family in the ratio of five to one, "down goes the

dust." A capital investment! Health and longevity, blooming cheeks, diminution of pill boxes, and physic bottles:-
Tis a consummation devoutly to be wish'd!
Let us see, how runs our calculation.

		£	s.	d.	£	s.	d.
40 Subscribers	at	0	10	6	21	0	0
30 „	at	1	1	0	31	10	0
10 „	at	2	2	0	21	0	0
10 „	at	3	3	0	31	10	0
10 „	at	5	5	0	52	10	0
5 „	at	10	10	0	52	10	0
		----			----		
105					210		

If the above sum could be raised, something handsome might be set apart for adornments- also for the purchase of an excellent telescope. Suppose, however, the expenses of fitting up is £105 which the following moderate number of subscribers would do:-

		£	s.	d.	£	s.	d.
20 Subscribers	at	0	10	6	10	10	0
15 „	at	1	1	0	15	15	0
6 „	at	2	2	0	12	12	0
6 „	at	3	3	0	18	18	0
5 „	at	5	5	0	26	5	0
2 „	at	10	10	0	21	0	0
		----			----		
54					105	0	0

Yours, &c.
A SUBSCRIBER.

17th July 1851
On Saturday last a meeting of the Ulverston subscribers to the National Testimonial, erected on the Hill of Hoad to the memory of our late distinguished townsman, Sir John Barrow, Bart., was

held to receive Sir George Barrow, Bart., and John Barrow Esq., F.R.S., who had been deputed by the London Committee to communicate to the subscribers here, their final resolutions as to the future disposal of the Tower. On the motion of Rev. R. Gwillym, seconded by Mr. John Barrow, Lieut. George H. C. Sutherland, R. N., was called to the chair, and there were present also the following subscribers:- Rev. Richard Gwillym, Mr. S. Soulby, Mr. Henry Dickinson, Mr. Henry Remington, Mr. T. T. Fell, Mr. T. Town, Mr. T. T. Briggs, Mr. J. H. Barrow, Mr. W. Salmon, Mr. M. Mawson, and Mr. Ainslie.

Before reading the resolutions of the London Committee, Sir George Barrow read over the amount of subscriptions for the Monument, and also the payments made out of it. The following are the resolutions adopted by the London Committee:-

"At a final meeting of the Committee of the Barrow Tower, held at the Admiralty, 1st July, 1851. Sir George T. Staunton, Bart., MP in the chair,-

"It was unanimously resolved that the Committee having received from Mr. Trimen, the architect, a statement of the erection of the Barrow Tower having being completed to his satisfaction, they consider that the charge which they undertook is now accomplished; and in relinquishing their duties, Mr. Barrow, of the Admiralty, having represented to them that his late father's family are desirous that the Trustees of the Town's Lands of Ulverston should hereafter have the charge of the building, they request that the secretary will convey a copy of this resolution to the Trustees of that place, with the expression of their anxiety that the wishes of the late Sir John Barrow's representatives may meet with their cordial attention, and that so costly an ornament as the Tower proves to be, to Ulverston and its vicinity, will become an object of their special care and preservation from the ravages of time; and that the efforts of the subscribers to perpetuate the memory of Sir John Barrow, at his native town, thus so effectually carried out, will be equally well seconded by his fellow-townsmen, not only from a respect to the feelings of his descendants, but also from an affectionate remembrance of his virtues and his excellencies.

The family of the late Sir John Barrow having placed at the disposal of the Committee, three separate keys to the Tower, it was resolved that they be forwarded to the Trustees of the Town's Lands of Ulverston, with a request that they will keep one for their own use, and place the second in the hands of the Incumbent of Ulverston, to remain always in that office, and the third in the hands of the tenant, who may hold the land on which the Tower is situated.

"The thanks of the meeting were then voted to their president, Sir George Staunton, for his kind and considerate conduct in the chair."

The following resolutions were, after some deliberation, unanimously and cordially passed by the meeting:-

On the motion of Mr. Henry Dickinson, seconded by Mr. S. Soulby, resolved that in reference to the resolutions (just read to the meeting) made at the Admiralty, on the 1st day of July, 1851, with respect to the future care and management of the late Sir John Barrow's Testimonial, that this meeting approves of the resolutions entered into on that day, and that the future care and management of the Barrow Testimonial be invested in the Trustees of the Town's Lands of Ulverston.

On the motion of Sir George Barrow, seconded by Mr. John Barrow, resolved that the Trustees of the Town's Lands should not be held answerable for any expenses which may remain to be incurred, in completion of the Barrow Testimonial, but that they be requested to adopt such measures as they may deem expedient to defray the expenses or charges still due.

On the motion of Lieut. Sunderland, seconded by Mr. Remington, resolved that a printed placard be posted and circulated, to deter parties from committing wilful injury and nuisance; and that a board be painted and posted up, with the following inscription- "Visitors are earnestly requested to respect this Monument, which has been erected as a National Testimony, in honour of the late Sir John Barrow, Baronet, a native of Ulverston."

Sir George Barrow and Mr. John Barrow each returned thanks to the Ulverston Committee and Subscribers, for their services and liberality.

Moved by the Rev. R. Gwillym that the best thanks of this Committee be returned to Sir Geo. Barrow, Mr. John Barrow, and other members of their family, for their great liberality towards the expenses of the National Testimonial.

Moved by Mr. T. T. Briggs that the best thanks of this meeting be given to Sir George Staunton, Bart., Capt. Beecher, and the rest of the London Committee, for their exertions.

Sir George Barrow and Mr. John Barrow expressed to the meeting the readiness with which Mr. Postlethwaite, the Lessee of the Town's Lands on which the National Testimonial stands, met the views and wishes of the London and Local Committees, as communicated to him by Sir George and Mr. John Barrow.

Moved by Mr. John Barrow, that the thanks of this meeting be given to Lieut. Sunderland, for his services in the chair.
Sir George Barrow and his brother repeatedly expressed their warm appreciation of the kindness with which they had been received at Ulverston, and for the interest which so many had taken in aiding the fund for erecting the Tower. We feel sure we are but expressing the sentiments of all who were present at the meeting, that Sir George and his brother, by their affability and courtesy, "won golden opinions from all."

17th July 1851
During the past week a series of annoyances and wanton mischief have been exercised upon the Barrow Monument in the absence

of the workmen, by breaking open the door, injuring the stone facings and committing nuisances. We have reason to believe that the offenders are a clique of thoughtless idle boys who in a true spirit of mischief have perpetrated these outrages; but let them beware of such proceedings in future, as a reward is advertised for the discovery of the guilty party. -Our adult population we are sure have too much respect for the monument, and the memory of him whom it is designed to honour, to raise a hand against it.

7th November 1851
Some thoughtless and mischievous person has been wantonly defacing the inscription place over the doorway leading to the interior of this edifice. We cannot too much deprecate such unmeaning and unmanly conduct; and we trust the perpetrators of such disgraceful acts will be found out and punished as they deserve.

15th April 1852
Easter Sunday.
The Hill of Hoad, on Sunday afternoon last, presented a most animated appearance. The day being remarkably fine -a cloudless sky -and the sun emitting, when at meridian height, quite a midsummer warmth, drew forth the bulk of our juvenile population to the place, large groups of whom might be seen scattered over the hill in every direction, eagerly engaged in the innocent annual diversion of rolling their party-coloured eggs, apparently absorbed in high enjoyment of this important and long anticipated day. It was calculated that there were not less than five hundred children engaged in this amusement at one time, either as principals or lookers-on. Some parties, however were not quite so laudably nor innocently engaged - a boy in the true spirit of enterprise "under difficulties," contrived, we understand, to gain access into the interior of the Barrow Monument through the window in the basement, and having effected this, affixed the end of a rope to the stove, threw the other end out of the window, and thus afforded a mode of more easy ingress to others who eagerly availed themselves of it, and commenced a somewhat hazardous series of experimental trips to the top of the Monument. To shew

the dangers to which our thoughtless youths have voluntarily exposed themselves at different times previously, in their adventurous freaks, we may state that boys have been seen walking round the cupola on the outside, and on one occasion a certain dare-devil had actually the temerity to stand on his head upon it; and whilst the Monument was in course of building a mere boy seized the end of a rope fixed to the scaffolding necessary for the erection of the cupola, and went 'hand-over-hand' by it to the top, and afterwards descended by the same means.

8th July 1852
Cost of the Tower
The following is an account of the expense incurred in erecting the monumental tower on the Hoad Hill:-

	£.	S.	d.
Original contract with Messrs. Smith and Appleyard for building the tower.	800	0	0
Repair of cupola, damaged by lightning.	136	4	0
Fitting the lightning conductor.	46	0	0
Expenses attending the ceremony of laying the first stone.	63	0	0
Expenses of band of the 52nd light infantry on the above occasion.	32	0	0
Erecting small wood booth, *Messrs, Brocklebank's Estimate.*	36	0	0
Engraving of the Monument, and printing of copies for subscribers.	37	12	6
Advertisements.	28	0	0
Inscription on the door and in the lantern, as charged by the Messrs. Brocklebank.	33	7	0
Total	£1,193	13	6

A.B. Becher, Commander, R. N.
Honorary Secretary.

Days for hoisting the line of battle ship's Union Jack, - at the Barrow tower -the flag having been presented by the Lords Commissioners of the Admiralty.
From 8am. Until sunset, viz:-

15th May, Anniversary of the day upon which the foundation stone of the tower was laid.
24th May, The Queen's birth-day or day appointed.
18th June, The Battle of Waterloo, which secured peace to Europe.
19th June, the day on which Sir John Barrow was born at Dragleybeck, A.D. 1764.
20th June, The Accession.
28th June, The Coronation.
26th Aug., Prince Albert's Birth-day.
21st Oct., The Battle of Trafalgar.
22nd Oct., Birth-day of Sir George Barrow, Bart.
9th Nov., Birth-day of the Prince of Wales.
21st Nov., Birth-day of the Princess Royal.
23rd Nov., (Half-mast high.) The day upon which Sir John Barrow departed this life.

In addition to the foregoing the flag is hoisted on the following anniversaries:- 1st March, St. David's day, -17th March, St. Patrick's day, - 23rd April, St. George's day, - 30th November, St. Andrew's day.

21st October 1852
£2 REWARD.
Whereas a very great amount of malicious Damage has at different times been done to the Monument to the memory of the late Sir John Barrow, on the Hill of Hoad, and particularly on or about the 4th inst., after the Monument had undergone a series of repairs, by making forcible entrance through one of the windows, injuring the framework thereof, and carrying away one of the iron bars; defacing the plaster work, splitting a panel of the door, and doing other damage to the Tower.

Notice is therefore hereby given, that the above reward will be paid by Superintendent Davidson, of the Police Office in this town, to any person who will give such information as will lead to the conviction of the Offender or Offenders.
Police Office, Ulverston,
October 18th 1852.

20th January 1853
To the Editor of *Soulby's Ulverston Advertiser*. Dear Sir, -Knowing your willingness to insert in the columns of your paper any communications which may tend to the improvement of our town and neighbourhood, I take the present opportunity of making a few remarks in reference to the neglected state of the Barrow Tower on Hoad; in the hope that any humble suggestion which I offer may be the means of getting it completed, and thereby rendering it, as originally intended, a place of attraction and resort. The lack of funds necessary for its completion is much to be regretted. The committee in London no doubt exceeded the limits of the original contract, which must be attributed to their anxiety to perpetuate the memory of a faithful servant of the country. This praiseworthy feeling ought to have been responded to by the inhabitants of Ulverston and the district. I cannot but think that it must be very disheartening to the family of the late Sir John Barrow (who subscribe to nearly all our charitable institutions) to know that the inhabitants of Ulverston have not a spirit of liberality in support of the memorial, which has been so niggardly encouraged by the people of Furness.

The monument, if completed, would be an object of great interest to visitors, and might be made at no great cost a place of resort to thousands. It will be necessary, however, before that can be done, to lay the floors, without which to ascend it, it is dangerous. The top portion requires glazing, and the outside cementing. This done, I would place in the interior geological specimens, a good telescope, &c; affording an attraction which might be the means of realizing a fund for repairs and improvements by a small charge to non-subscribers for ascending the tower. The opening next summer might be celebrated by a fancy fair on the hill, which would be both novel and attractive.

The lessee of the land on which the tower is built is, I am sure, as anxious as myself for its completion, and would, I am convinced, co-operate with the Ulverston committee in affecting this desirable object.

I have only to add, in conclusion, that it is anything but attractive in its present state, and is fast falling to decay.
Yours. &c., A SUBSCRIBER.

27th January 1853
To the Editor of *Soulby's Ulverston Advertiser*. Sir,- Your dolorous correspondent, on the subject of the Barrow Monument, last week, provokes a smile at his philosophy. To be sure, decay is inherent in everything around us, not on the monument only, but on all other buildings in the town and neighbourhood. His morbid feelings, on matters so very imperfectly understood, would lead your numerous readers to suppose his assertions are facts. It might be more upon a level with his knowledge, if he had informed the admirers of the Barrow Monument, that those beautiful foot walks, up the hill, have perceptibly decayed, and should, this spring, have the slight repairs they require. Had his bright understanding suggested a more convenient road from the town to the foot of Hoad, we might have had the benefit of so well informed a mind.
January 24th, 1853.
L. R. C.

10th February 1853
To the Editor of the *Ulverston Advertiser*. Sir,- My attention has been called to a letter signed "Subscriber," in your journal of the 20th ultimo, on the subject of the neglected state of the Barrow Tower. Whoever the "Subscriber" may be I thank him for his kind feeling and friendly intentions, and particularly for the public spirit he has evinced.

I am desirous, however, of saying a few words in respect to his remarks that "the Committee in London no doubt exceeded the limit of the original contract, &c.," if allowed to pass unnoticed, it might leave the subscribers to the Monument under an erroneous impression, which I am sure is not the wish of that gentleman.

The original contract with Messrs. Smith and Appleford was strictly adhered to by the Committee. The amount was £800, which was paid in instalments, as the work progressed, and under certificates that the work was properly executed.

The cupola was damaged by lightning, and Messrs. Brocklebank, who built the Tower, repaired it for £136 4s having taken the upper part down very near, I believe, to the coping stone, which projects from the building. The family bore the greater part of this expense.

A lightning conductor was fixed which cost £46. An inscription over the door and in the lanthorn was cut by my order, and for which I paid Messrs. Brocklebank (through their attorney Mr. Yarker) and from my own private funds, the goodly sum of £32 that covered that work. I am now on the point of paying the aforesaid Messrs. Brocklebank, (through the aforesaid attorney) a further goodly sum of £49 17s 2d, for erecting and removing a small booth, which accommodated a few of the gentry of Ulverston, their families, and ourselves, on the occasion of the ceremony of laying the first stone. More than half this sum will also be paid from my own private funds. I suppose timber is dear in the neighbourhood, and labor high, as I find that works of a similar description in London, but *capable of accommodating ten times the number of people*, are erected at a third less than the cost of this "Pavilion," the name by which the booth was signified in Messrs. Brocklebank's bill.

It would take up too much space to go into further details, suffice to say that I have personally expended a great deal more from my own private funds, and have just paid for a beautifully carved centre stone, which any one may see at Mr. Young's, the sculptor, but which I have caused to be inserted in the dome of the lower apartments, because the mortar of the bricks is as moist as the day it was made, from the constant wet which pours through the walls of the tower from top to bottom.

I must apologise for the length of this letter, but it is due to the Committee in London to state these facts for the information of the inhabitants of Ulverston.

I am, Sir, Your very humble servant, John Barrow.
London, 2nd. February, 1853.

17th February 1853
To the Editor of the *Ulverston Advertiser*. Sir, -As Mr. Barrow has in his letter on the subject of the "Barrow Tower," which appeared in your last paper week's paper, thought proper to introduce our names in a manner which deem calculated to prejudice us as builders and tradesmen, we feel called upon to offer a few remarks by way of explanation and reply.

It appears that some person has in a former letter, chosen to find fault with the unfinished state of the Tower, and that Mr. Barrow in recapitulating the various sums he has already disbursed towards its erection,- by way of apology, we suppose, for suffering it to remain in its present neglected condition -has thought fit to refer, amongst other things, to a sum of £49 17s 2d, which (as he says) we compelled him to pay through our attorney, Mr. Yarker, for erecting what we grieve to find he is offended at our dignifying by the name of a *Pavilion*, for the accommodation of the public, when the foundation stone of the building was laid-as if he had been unjustly called upon to pay it, and the amount were unfair and excessive.

It is, no doubt, well known that we built the Tower by contract. We do not, however, collect from Mr. Barrow's letter, that it is pretended that the erection of this "*Pavilion*" formed any part of the contract work. The fact is, we undertook its erection, under the special order of two of the most active and influential members of the committee, and it was not until we had repeatedly, but in vain, sought payment through them, that we ventured to apply to Mr. Barrow. Our application to him, however, we are sorry to say, met with no better success. Our bill, which amounted to £35 10s 11d only, was stigmatised as an imposition. Payment was withheld, and not until after numerous pressing applications, and divers gentle threats did our attorney succeed in prevailing on Mr. Barrow, through his architect, Mr. Trimen, to allow the compensation to which we were entitled, to be settled by arbitration.

For the purpose of effecting this arrangement an architect of eminence, residing in Liverpool, was mutually fixed upon by both parties as sole referee, and a statement, containing the particulars of the work was we had performed, was laid before him. Each party drew up such written explanations as he pleased, in support of his own side of the case, and these, after having being submitted to and approved of by the opposite party, were laid before the architect for his consideration, the result was, an award in our favor, whereby the arbitrator fixed the value of our work not at the sum of £35 10s 11d., the amount of our bill *as priced by ourselves,* but at the sum of £49 17s 2d., £14 6s 3d, more than our original charge.

On receiving this award, it was immediately transmitted to Mr. Trimen by Mr. Yarker. This produced a letter to him from Mr. Barrow, complaining of the decision, but offering (though it must be admitted with a very bad grace) to pay the £35 10s 11d.

This offer, however, "the attorney aforesaid" very properly refused, and after a somewhat angry correspondence between him and Mr. Barrow, the latter paid the full amount awarded to us.

From this statement we think the public will be able to see, that whoever may be in the wrong, we have been more "sinned against than sinning."

As it may probably be suggested that we ought to have enforced payment from the gentlemen of the Local Committee, who personally ordered the work to be done, rather than from Mr. Barrow, we may observe, that we were advised by our attorney (the attorney aforesaid) that it would not be fair to resort to our legal claim on them, until every endeavour to obtain the money, from those equitably bound to discharge it, had been tried, and failed. This course, no doubt, was a more expensive one for us, but whatever Mr. Barrow may think, we feel quite satisfied, we did right in adopting it.

With regard to the bill, to which Mr. Barrow alludes, relative to the inscription, we have little to say; Mr. Barrow ordered it, and we appealed to him for payment of our charge, as a matter of course. He certainly did oblige us to resort to the interference of our attorney to recover it, but as he ultimately settled the amount, there is an end of the matter, as far as we are concerned.

As we have been brought before the public, we hope we may be excused for availing ourselves of the opportunity, which it affords us, of proclaiming that we have other demands for work done by us, respecting this unfortunate Tower, which we have not been able to get satisfied, and for the recovery of which we fear we shall be driven to adopt legal proceedings, unless this public announcement shall, as we sincerely hope it may, have the effect of inducing the defaulter or defaulters to do us tardy justice.

We are, Sir, your obedient humble servants.

J. & W. BROCKLEBANK.

24th February 1853

To the Editor of the *Ulverston Advertiser*. Sir, -On the subject of Messrs. J. and W Brocklebank's letter, in your last number, permit me to observe that it was not the justice of their claim to payment of a reasonable charge for the erection of the so called *pavilion* to which I objected, but to what I considered the unreasonable extravagance of their charge.

It is true the claim itself was an unexpected one to me when first made, but it did not surprise me nearly so much as the amount claimed; -for seeing that no part of the materials employed in the work by Messrs. Brocklebank had, I understand, been left on the ground, but that all had been removed by them, it certainly did appear to me that £35 10s 11d. was a very exorbitant charge for simply the use of the materials, putting up, taking down, and removing the same; and I think that any disinterested persons who were present at the ceremony of laying the foundation stone of the Barrow Tower, and who have any recollection of Messrs. Brocklebank's *pavilion*, will agree with me on that point. My opinion was however, strengthened by the opinions of more competent judges than myself in such matters, who told me that the charge ought not, under the circumstances, to have exceeded £15, or £20 at the outside.

Messrs. Brocklebank's attorney, Mr. Yarker, was accordingly remonstrated with on the subject, in the hope of obtaining some deduction of the charge; but without effect. On the contrary, the matter having been referred to a third party, at the suggestion, I believe, of the aforesaid attorney, I have been compelled to pay to the Messrs. Brocklebank the still larger sum of £49 17s 2d., being £14 6s 3d more than in the original bill.

With the propriety of their attorney in having "very properly refused" to receive the amount of their original demand, and insisted upon payment of the *additional* sum of £14 6s 3d. the Messrs. Brocklebank may congratulate themselves, -but I think the public will easily perceive the reason why!

It is not my intention to enter into any further correspondence on this subject.

I am. Sir, your most obedient servant. John Barrow.
London, 21st. Feb., 1853.

3rd March 1853
To the Editor of the *Ulverston Advertiser.* Sir. -May I ask through your columns, if it has been determined, either by the Ulverston Committee, or the Committee in London, to make any effort to raise funds for the completion of the tower on the Hill of Hoad, erected to the memory of the late Sir John Barrow? I shall not trouble you or your readers by entering into a discussion as whether the private virtues or public services of the deceased Baronet merited the erection of a public monument- it is enough for my purpose, that the shell of a monument has been erected, and that it has been left for nearly two years in a state that reflects no small discredit upon the inhabitants of Ulverston.

That I am actuated by no interested or sinister motive, I may mention, that I have not been a contributor, nor shall I think of becoming one, until I see something like a stir made, to make the Barrow Monument what it ought to be, an object of interest to our locality.

Apart, then from all consideration as to the motive which first prompted its erection I have only to observe that as the building -I cannot call it a Monument -is there, let us do our best to make it worthy of inspection, not only for the inhabitants of our district, but for strangers. To do this, the interior must be thoroughly finished, and made attractive - the base surrounded by an iron railing, and the ascent from the high road improved.

If the present Ulverston Committee will not act, or will not exert themselves, to carry out these improvements, let them resign and others be chosen to fill their places. To raise the funds necessary for these purposes, would, I think, be a difficult matter. Let a penny-subscription be opened, and a subscription list for parties desirous of availing themselves of a life-right to admission to the tower. From these sources, and the annual income arising from the sale of tickets, there can be little fear but ample means would be derived to defray the expense of completing the tower, and to lay by a yearly sum for necessary repairs.
Yours, &c., AN ULVERSTONIAN.

4th May 1854
John & Wm. Brocklebank v. Geo. Smith and Jacob Appleford.
This was an action to recover the balance of an account. The original claim was £50 8s. 3.1/2 d., but the plaintiffs abandoned as excel the 8s 3.1/2d. The plaintiffs, on the 16th of May, 1850, entered into an agreement with the defendants, (who were the contractors for the erection of the Barrow Tower on the hill of Hoad, near this town,) to build the tower according to certain plans and sections furnished to them. The total amount of the contract was £525 5s. The following is a copy of the plaintiffs' bill of particulars:-

£ s. d.

April 27th,- 1850.- To 72.1/2 cubic yards
of extra foundation wall, made perfectly solid

with large stones and mortar, grouted at 8s.-6d.	30	16	3
May 16th.- Amount of contract, for the mason's work, and walling of the "Barrow Tower," on the Hill of Hoad, near Ulverston.	525	5	0
To allowance for taking down and rebuilding a certain portion of wall as per agreement.	10	0	0
Aug 2nd.-To extra strong malleable iron ramp for supporting the ends of stone steps in the spiral staircase per order of Mr. Mackland and not included in the contract, (substituted in place of 200 ½ feet brick wall in contract.)	4	13	3
August 12th,- To strong oak timber for plate pieces for the guiders, and hoop iron bond, not in contract.	10	17	1½
Sept. 3rd.- To making alterations in the buttress of building, in order to get a manhole, (which was afterwards disannulled,) including taking down a large portion of wall, breaking into buttress, making good the same, centering, &c. Per order of Mr. Mackland.	3	15	11½
Novr. 15th.-To repairs of "Tower," damages to scaffolding, &c., occasioned by tempest, Nov. 4th, 1850.	16	11	8
May 17th, 1851.- To masons boring holes in the steps of staircase for the smith to fix his iron balusters to per order of Mr. Mackland	2	16	3
July 12th. —Assisting to fix door frames per order of Mr. Mackland	0	11	6
Assisting the plumbers, boring hole for water pipe, &c., &c., per order Mr. Mackland	2	11	3
Sept 1st. -To work, and materials in forming a cement cornice, round living room, (not included in the contract,) per order Mr. Mackland.	6	8	6
	£614.6.		9.

By cash received on account in 4 payments	539	0	1
Allowance for 200 feet ½ brick wall (unexecuted but in contract.)	5	0	0
Allowance respecting brick arch, unexecuted	14	2	0
Do. For steps to basement, do	4	13	4½
Do. For setting in brickwork, a small stove	1	3	0
	563	18	3½
	£50	8	3½

The first item in this account was an agreement at the price stated between them and Mr. Hughes, the defendants' clerk, and which work was completed before the agreement with the defendants was entered into. The defendants allowed at the rate of 5s. per cubic yard, and the plaintiffs charged 8s. 6d, the question, therefore, was what is a fair and reasonable charge; but the defendants positively swore that they agreed for 8s. 6d. This made a difference of £12 13s. 9d. Mr Thompson, architect, of Kendal, spoke to the value of the work. The second and third items were not disputed. The fourth item was a charge for an iron ramp for staircase, which was ordered by Mr. Mackland, an assistant of Mr. Trimen, the architect for the work, in the place of 200 ½ feet brick wall, but no portion of the brick wall was executed, although the defendants allowed for 162 feet, and the difference between the charge for ramp and allowance by defendants for brick wall was 12. 3d. The fifth item was not disputed. The sixth item was extra work, and done and replaced by Mr. Mackland's order. The seventh item was occasioned by storm, and it was alleged that the agreement provide for it, but it was contended for the defence, that the scaffolding had not been properly and securely put up,
-that the ropes were bad, but the assertions were not substantiated. The eight and ninth items were not disputed. The tenth item was not shewn in the plan, or bill of quantities. The eleventh item was for extra work, and for work ordered by Mr. Mackland. The case was heard at great length, and at the conclusion his Honor gave a verdict for the first item £12 13s. 9d.; allowed £8 5s 10d. for the damage done by storm, and £3 for the eleventh item; making

altogether £23 19s. 7d. For the sixth item, he thought the architect was liable, and they could sue either Mr. Mackland or Mr. Trimen. The tenth item he held was within the contract, and did not allow it.

1st June 1854

Report on activity in the Barrow Monument:- The Armorial bearings of the late Sir John Barrow, Bart., by Mr G. H. Young, of this town, sculptor, were placed yesterday upon the exterior of the Barrow Monument, immediately over the door-way.

The Arms are sculptured out of one solid block of Birkrigg-stone, leaving the Squirrel and Helmet, which are beautifully cut, entirely naked, and free from the back-ground of the stone. The Ulster hand is exquisitely executed, and the workmanship altogether, reflects the highest credit on the artist, and forms besides, a great ornamental addition to the tower. It is to be hoped that every respectable inhabitant will observe a strict surveillance in preserving this additional memorial of the late respected baronet, in its exposed situation, from mischievous evil doers, which, it is well known, this tower has not altogether heretofore escaped. Sir George Staunton, a venerable friend of the family, (son of the late Sir George Staunton, who in his early days, the late Sir John Barrow accompanied on his emissary to China,) visited the monument on Tuesday last, and expressed himself highly gratified at its appearance, and with the excellent condition, which, after its late renovation, it now presents.

10th August 1854
Mashiter V Afflick

The plaintiff, a twine spinner in this town, sued the defendant for £1/0s/3d., being the amount of his charge for a colour-rope supplied for the use of the Barrow monument. He stated that having instructions from defendant to make a rope for the purpose of hoisting a flag on the monument, to be charged to Sir George Barrow, he completed the order, but on applying to Sir George for the amount of his account he was informed that no one had been authorised by him to give this order, and that he (plaintiff) must look to the party who ordered the rope for the payment of his account. He had, therefore, been compelled to sue the defendant, he having ordered the rope, which was 36 yards in length, and of a peculiar make, having a copper wire passed down the middle, for which he charged 5¾d per yard, amounting to the sum of £1 0s. 3d.

Defendant did not dispute ordering the rope, but alleged that plaintiff had made an extortionate demand, being six times the value of the rope. He produced various samples from other masters, which appeared thicker and better rope, the price of which was 1d. per yard. He also called upon Henry Crewdson, foreman to the Messrs. Hartley, who stated that 1d. per yard was quite sufficient. When asked if the copper wire made any difference, he stated that if plaintiff introduced it without special orders, he ought to have 3¼d. per yard less; but, if ordered, that much more.

His honor therefore reduced the account to 4s. 6d. and gave an immediate order for the amount.

October 1855
SIR JOHN BARROW, BART., -The splendid bust of the deceased, by our townsman Mr. Young, and which recently received high commendation from the *Art Journal,* is now placed in its permanent resting, the Barrow Tower on the hill of Hoad.

October 9th 1856
Lady Franklin, widow of the lamented and celebrated artic voyager, Sir john Franklin, accompanied by her niece Miss Sophia Crancroft, paid a visit to the Barrow Monument on her way to the lakes on Monday last. Her Ladyship ascended to the top of the tower with the utmost activity, where she remained for nearly an hour, in company of Miss Crancroft, and the custodian, the latter of whom she detained the whole time, asking him innumerable questions relative to the locality; land compass in hand marking the bearings and making a sketch. The day being remarkably fine and clear, Lancaster could be discerned very plainly in the distance with the naked eye. The several mansions of the neighbouring

gentry were noticed by her, and the names of the owners enquired of the custodian, together with the rivers and other striking objects. In honour of her ladyships visit the flag on the monument was kept flying till Tuesday evening, the time of her departure, to Newby Bridge, previous to which, however, she paid a visit to the Infants' School and the Parish Church.

22nd Jan 1858
THE ROYAL MARRAGE.
Ulverston showed its loyalty on this occasion by keeping Monday as a holiday. Business was entirely suspended, and merry peals were rung on the bells of the parish church at intervals during the day. The Barrow monument was gaily decked with flags, and we think we may safely add, that a universal feeling prevailed, at least if we may judge from the hearty wishes which were expressed for the health and happiness of the royal pair. -We have also much pleasure in recording that, of the ladies, working members of the Ulverston Dorcas Institute, who spent a very pleasant evening in the large room of the Savings' Bank in honor of the happy event. Among other excellent edibles we may mention a large ornamented bride's cake. We need hardly add that the health and happiness of the royal bride and bridegroom was the expressed and heartfelt wish of all present.

29th April 1858
WANTON MISCHIEF.
Last week some evilly disposed individual maliciously broke one of the windows in the Barrow monument, by throwing two stones through the same. The window mentioned is not less than 30 feet from the ground, and the stones are not less than half a pound weight, so that no child could throw them. The mouldings outside the door have also been cut; and two seats on Hoad torn up and taken away. What can induce the perpetration of such malpractices as these we are at a loss to divine. The monument stands there to perpetuate the memory of one who raised himself from the rank of humble life to that of great eminence, and we think the very knowledge of the fact would suffice to stay the hand of the most ignorant and wickedly disposed from mutilating it, but such

appears not to be the fact; there is, it appears, amongst us even in this enlightened age those who are so prone to vice that they cannot pass a dumb monument without indulging their disreputable propensities. A reward is offered and we sincerely trust that the miscreant, whoever he may be, will be brought to justice and meet with his just dessert.

24th March 1859
Treat To School Children.
On Tuesday last the children of the Barrow National School, accompanied by their teachers, were conveyed by train to Ulverston, and after a trip to the Barrow Monument, were taken to the Concert Hall, to hear Dr. Mark and his little men. All were much pleased with the excursion, and expressed by frequent cheers the delight they experienced in the enjoyment provided for them, as, also, for the slight, but grateful repast of oranges and biscuits so liberally provided by their several lady, and other friends. For the day's holiday, and its consequent pleasures, the juveniles are mainly indebted to James Ramsden, Esq,; but, secondarily, to the kind contributors to the *refreshment fund*. Not the slightest accident occurred; and, on their return, all cheered heartily for their several friends, and departed to their respective homes.

29th September 1859
THE BARROW MONUMENT AND THE HILL OF HOAD.
To the Editor of the *Ulverston Advertiser.* Sir.- It is to be regretted that the Hill of Hoad with the Barrow Monument is not better known to tourists. The sight or prospect from the tops of the lake mountains do not afford anything so picturesque as the scenery which opens to the view from the top of Hoad. It is not my intention to enlarge upon what might be done by the Inhabitants of Ulverston, assisted by the gentry of the district, in converting that delightful hill to a pleasure ground, and by obtaining leave (which would surely be granted) from Mr. John Barrow, to make the Monument serve the purpose of a Walhalla or Valhalla for the district. How many worthies Furness has sent forth may be learned from any guide-book, and small tablets, where busts are not obtainable, might be fixed upon the walls to their memory. The

hill I was informed belongs to the parish; let it be converted by the trustees with the consent of the Lord Chancellor and a vestry meeting to a purpose that would bring in a revenue more than treble the best rent that can now be got for it, by making it attractive to the district and an inducement to tourists to linger a few days in Ulverston, for around the town there are many beauties truly worth seeing which are not mentioned in the numerous guide-books.
Yours, &c
A Cockney. London, September. 1859.

Conclusion

From September 1859 *The Soulby Ulverston Advertiser* ceased to report news of the Barrow Monument. I have searched, without success, to find an announcement of the grand opening. It seems sad and strange that the interest and enthusiasm for the building of the monument should have waned to this extent.

During my tenure as Caretaker on Hoad, Bill O'Neill, the Town Clerk in Ulverston, gave me a copy of some notes he had written while researching the life of Sir John Barrow; I thought it would be appropriate to include them here as a footnote.
JL

'In 1864, Robert Hanney of Springfield, and Mr. Brogden of Holme Island, bought, from Dr. Gilpin, the Cottage and Garden at Dragley Beck where Sir John Barrow was born, and presented it to John Barrow. Then on September 14th 1895, John Barrow offered the Cottage and land to the Ulverston Urban District Council, along with two Albums relating to the Monument's plans, sketches and lists of subscribers, also many original letters and newspaper reports. (These Albums are now in the safe custody of the Cumbria County Council Archives, and can be withdrawn by the Town Council at any time.)

Sir John Barrow last saw his native Town in 1796, at the age of 32 years, and when he wrote his autobiography at the age of 82 years, he said that nearly all the people he had known in Ulverston had died. He also said that the only doctor he had ever consulted was a Chinese Physician 50 years earlier. He wrote volumes on his travels in China, South Africa, also a Chronological History of Artic Voyages, and Voyages and Discoveries into the Artic Regions. He lists 195 articles in the "Quarterly Review" and 12 in "Encyclopaedia Britannica."

On Monday, May 15th, 1950, Ulverston Townspeople paid tribute to Sir John by marking the Centenary of the laying of the Foundation Stone. Hundreds of people gathered on Hoad Hill and watched the Chairman of the Council, Mr. Henry Simpson, break the Union Flag, which was presented for the occasion by the Admiralty. Mr. Harry Birkett, J.P. delivered the oration, which was on the life and work of Sir John.'